T0120967

HOW TO FIND THE PERFECT LOVE

STEP BY STEP GUIDE TO A FRUITFUL, FULFILLING, AND HEALTHY RELATIONSHIP

DARRELL CANTY

HOW TO FIND THE PERFECT LOVE
STEP BY STEP GUIDE TO A FRUITFUL, FULFILLING, AND HEALTHY RELATIONSHIP

iUniverse books may be ordered through booksellers or by contacting:

iUniverse
1663 Liberty Drive
Bloomington, IN 47403
www.iuniverse.com
844-349-9409

Because of the dynamic nature of the Internet, any web addresses or links contained in this book may have changed since publication and may no longer be valid. The views expressed in this work are solely those of the author and do not necessarily reflect the views of the publisher, and the publisher hereby disclaims any responsibility for them.

Any people depicted in stock imagery provided by Getty Images are models, and such images are being used for illustrative purposes only. Certain stock imagery © Getty Images.

ISBN: 978-1-6632-2934-2 (sc)
ISBN: 978-1-6632-2933-5 (e)

Library of Congress Control Number: 2021919602

Print information available on the last page.

iUniverse rev. date: 06/20/2023

To several wonderful women who've deeply inspired me and aided my growth, helping me to become a better person, sincerely, warmly, and with great gratitude. Raeshawn Gaines, Sylvia Nicolis, and Regina Jackson, you've significantly affected my life and motivated me to understand the true concept of relationships. And to my father God, with utmost and superior gratitude, for everything to him be the glory.

CONTENTS

ACKNOWLEDGMENTS

I wish to recognize the many people I've met and experienced on my journey through life who've moved me with a passion to learn from them, to help them, and to receive help from them. Our relationships have helped me to better understand the natural functions of men and women It has been a personal commitment and inspiration to pursue.

PREFACE

I was moved many years ago to try to understand relationships between men and women, mainly for my benefit. Over years of carefully observing the people around me, I came to realize that most of us didn't have a clue. Every person I encountered, observed and later spoke with about his or her relationship or marriage didn't have a clear understanding of how each person should function to be at their best in their relationship. Many of these people didn't even know how to get the best out of their relationship for themselves. Through asking many questions and studying different behaviors, I discovered that men and women share many of the same behavior struggles. Many couples lack the understanding of how they should conduct themselves to get the best out of themselves or their partner. Most men and women don't know how to facilitate a healthy relationship and, here we are!

If you are single, have a boyfriend or girlfriend, a son or daughter, a mother or father, or someone who is engaged in any type of relationship, this book is designed for you. It will enable you to take on a new perspective on relating and how it was intended for us to relate with ourselves and others. The information in *How to Find the Perfect Love* is designed to benefit any type of relationship—relationships with friends, coworkers, neighbors, dating partners, and on and on. And it's intended to deliver a clear vision of how people were meant to communicate, interact, and behave with one another and with themselves, to get a healthy result.

I've been seeking to understand relationships, primarily those between men and women, for the past twenty-plus years. It has been a hunger, and an ongoing desire of mine, and this book has a Christian perspective.

Many of life's relationship experiences, as well as men's and women's natural nature to relate, are revealed here. This is to help us understand and transformed a better outcome in relationships. I hope readers will have a clear perspective on how to successfully incorporate this information into their personal lives. The focus primarily is on an individual understanding the natural way to be an intact and unbroken person, functioning separately from a couple in a relationship or codependency on others. The book also addresses how to connect to and relate with a well-fit, rational mental and emotional understanding of self and why one should select an attitude of willingness to effectively relate with others.

INTRODUCTION

Broken People Make broken relationships.

Most of our controllable good fortunes or tragedies we experience as humans are surrounded by or a product of some form of relationship. What befalls us is related to emotional, domestic, or materialistic partnerships whether it's legal or illegal involvement with the law, or not. All controllable experiences are directly linked to the results of a healthy or dysfunctional relationship. When behavior is dysfunctional, it stimulates people's incompatibility and inability to give healthy emotional and mental responses to life's situations. All of us around the world have been touched or affected by such tragedies or know someone who has. *How to Find the Perfect Love* slowly reveals how and why people behave this way. It also uncovers how broken people can recover and function as they were intended to function.

I've seen and experienced the scars and hurt of broken relationships. The animosity, bitterness, and hatred result in and affect the internal walls of individuals and families. In addition, such experiences can move some people to afflict negativity on others—sometimes hundreds or even thousands in society—with their unhealthy behaviors, the very behaviors that are behind undeveloped and broken relationships.

Relationships are the most important factor in every person's life. Our relationships affect us in every area of our lives, both interpersonal and intrapersonal. Therefore, it is very important that we acquire this information and learn to understand our natural state. That way, we can consciously play a role in healing both ourselves and the social destruction among us all. Understanding the misbehaviors among us, learning how people are intended to function at their best, and knowing how to deal with people at their worst are the keys to solving all social difficulties. Hopefully, *How to Find the Perfect Love* will reveal a clear understanding of how we're truly meant to relate to one another. Also, outline a path that we can follow, and the actions we can take to engage in meaningful, healthy relationships.

The cultural "norms" of behavior are perpetuated through media like TV, news, books, the internet, and other forms. It's not unusual to see, hear, or act in ways that are unhealthy, engaging in behaviors informed by self-gratitude, anger, jealousy, greed, violence, and so on. This is what our culture demonstrates to be normal behavior every day conducting ourselves and even to be expected. It's normal within our culture, but it's not normal according to our natural nature. *How to Find the Perfect Love* will guide us through our culture's "normal" functioning way of relating and how people are conditioned to think about and accept these norms. This information will clarify how people were truly designed to function as a man to a woman and a woman to a man. Also, how to understand and discover true love, and true healthy couples.

CHAPTER 1

WHY DO PEOPLE BEHAVE THIS WAY?

The media has influenced us, teaching us that normal behavior can be defined as any behavior that's accepted or typical of any pattern that fits in with others—or not. What? There are so many different levels of what is "normal" because there is no one set example of what social norms are. Society no longer establishes today's social norms; rather, we're told, "Just be you."

Other than societal norms like obeying laws, enrolling kids in school, working, and adhering to common natural laws, society has walked away from its responsibility. There are no more community examples of healthy social human behavior when it comes to rational interactions between people. Many may believe that society has abandoned the concept of normal or healthy social interaction altogether and just accepts that the individual within all of us is unique. This concept has trickled down into all facets of our relationships today—which has a huge impact on healthy behavior in everyday life and relationships.

Being unique doesn't mean excusing or ignoring one's behavior. Rather, to honor uniqueness is to accept that a person is exceptional just as they are. Mainstream media has conditioned many people to believe that uniqueness is found in detail like hair and clothes and so on, along with attitudes and behaviors, and that we must accept each person to embrace their uniqueness. A person's hair, clothes, and other exterior expressions are just ways in which they're being different thru visual expression.

Yes, people should accept others for their differences, those given examples are not unique. Our behavior, though, is derived from a mindset based on a set of principles. Bad, unhealthy, or disruptive behavior should not be considered unique.

Many may not accept or practice this paradigm. It's not easy to make this distinction. And it's not typical in today's culture to function in challenging situations with a rational emotional and mental attitude. Becoming a healthy, whole person is key to experiencing the best life and developing a fruitful and fulfilling relationship with anyone. For many reasons, most people were never taught this. The main reason is that our culture's focus has been conditioned by the mainstream pressures of social economics. "The social rat race" focuses on finding opportunities and becoming competitive in the search for that "American dream"—a dream of reaching the materialistic success bar—and never focusing on wholly developing oneself, for self, or even recognizing the true value of self.

I thank you for allowing me to walk you through it. This has truly been a life's journey and a lifetime of longing, for me. May God bless the readers and followers of this unalterable wealth of information; may it be applicable in your life and in your loved ones' lives.

CHAPTER 2

PEOPLE DO WHAT'S EASY.

Most of us are accustomed to what we see and hear to be the norm. Many are conditioned to take the easiest route in life and to find someone to be in a relationship with. Many people, including myself, have been conditioned to gravitate to what is easiest and quickest. We are accustomed to buying things and doing things that make life easier. Most people will listen to almost anyone who can point them toward or lead them in that direction. For this reason, in relationships, most will choose the many easily broken roads that lead to separation, hurt, pain, dysfunction, and regret.

online dating

So, what is the easiest way to connect to one another today? Yes, you've guessed it—the internet. Our culture has developed a complete society on social media. In this separate e-world, which separates us from our real world, it's easy to meet, easy to hook up with, and easy to cheat. It's easy to be someone who you're not and easy to manipulate, invite in, and get involved in other people's lives. Please be careful rather than sorry when you involve your life with social media in this way.

catfishing

Catfishing involves doing what is easy, but not what's ethical. One of the biggest concerns of online dating is being catfished. This is because we desire an easy and right-now way to meet good-looking and well-off people. Society and the media teach many of us to be self-important and materialistic; the need for self-gratification is usually the highest on our priority list, we're told, "You deserve it," "Treat yourself," "Do you," "It's all about you," or "Love them but love you more." This type of mind mostly promotes self-gratification and self-centeredness. Most of us aren't taught true love or to have a high self-value or to value others with the most importance.

This may make it easy for many people to engage in behaviors like catfishing. This type of person may feel justified in using someone else's picture or information to lure others to satisfy their desires for pleasure-seeking. Online, it's easy to pretend you're someone you're not or say you have the things you don't. The internet provides a wall between you and reality; it's like the internet is saying, "Look at all that space between you, them, and the truth. They're thinking, they won't know." This mindset may give a person a sense of confidence and the ability to deceive with no immediate danger, threat, or consequences. When dating or engaging in interactions online, there is no need for courage or even honesty, because being online makes it easy to hide or conceal things, like transparency and the truth.

electronic communications

In addition, texting, messaging, or other forms of electronic communication provide a certain distance, and convenience when it comes to being deceitful. These methods of interacting make for a

4

nonpersonal connection and can mask the true intent of their intentions and communication. Meeting in person may well be something of the pastime of basic communication but recommended. It is much harder to be deceitful when speaking over the phone or in person.

If or when someone is not being transparent with you when dating or engaging with you online, electronic communications allow them time to build up a relationship connection with you before you meet. Their hope may be the connection will make you feel that you have something invested (time or feelings, for example) and have an established relationship when the truth comes out. Be careful. You should develop a certain set of rules or boundaries before you engage online with too much of your feeling, time, and money.

***

Doing what's easy may also come into play when it comes to feeling most people must have someone in their lives to feel complete. Because of this, many people go from one relationship to another when something is not working out so, as not to feel that loneliness or to just avoid being single. Many people are taught or told the need to be with someone is usually stronger than their desire to have a healthy relationship. When you don't have a standard of principles or your set of values is low, this behavior becomes easy and dangerous. This is what leads people to the belief that it's "better to have half a man or woman than nothing at all." This mindset may eventually prove destructive and hurtful to one or both parties involved. It also makes it easy to start another relationship while involved with someone or before ending the one you're in—to avoid being without one.

Others may see themselves as not picky or having low expectations, which allows them to be or remain in a relationship that's not necessarily satisfying. Or maybe they're just looking for a helpmate. Meaning, help me, and I'll be your mate. Many people find it very easy to get involved via electronic forms of communication. Some may be thinking, *If I'm less needy, it will be easier for someone to love me and accept me.* Or they plan to say and do what the other wants to get in good with him or her—and then they can be themselves, in person. Especially if their previous experiences have taught them that this mindset makes it easy to find partners, they may repeat this process until they think they have found the one.

What does Sex Mean?

Hooking up today is what many call dating, and it seems sex is on everyone's mind. Most women equate participating in sex with some form of security, affection, bonding, love, or control. While most men equate sex with sex. Some men may equate sex with a boost to their ego. Other men may see sex as a form of ownership or a woman desiring them as an opportunity to score, or just have a good time. Most times, sex for men is just sex. Many times, sex doesn't end up having the same meaning to men and women. Always have a talk before you engage in sex.

It begins easily enough, but the longer people participate in sleeping around or even with the same person without having a clear understanding of each other's intentions or the purpose of their sexual encounters, chaos, and dysfunction are sure to follow. Without knowing the purpose or expectations of connecting on this level will usually end in disparity, short-term, or disaster. When a relationship is founded on the strength of sexual bonds as the premise, it will not work! Sex is designed to reproduce and deliver a momentary fulfillment of satisfaction, not determine, or sustain feelings, commitment, or a relationship!

Most People are conditioned to think.

Most people are conditioned to believe relationships show them how to love and how to be loved. Many may believe relationships show who they want to be in life and who they don't want to be. There are those who rely on having a good relationship to allow them to truly be their true selves. Some people depend on relationships to increase their emotional well-being or at least make it better. A lot of people turn to relationships to create stability in their lives.

Some people are taught at an early age how to be a good friend or friendly to others and dependent on others but not how to be good to themselves. Most people are taught the importance of having someone to count on and someone to trust in times of need. More importantly, they are taught the great need to have someone by their side when facing hardships, big life challenges, and times of loneliness.

Almost none of us are taught that the most important relationship in our life is with ourselves. We aren't shown how to face hardships and life's big challenges with ourselves, how to love ourselves through difficulties, how to be emotionally stable when facing demanding situations, and how to count on ourselves and manage our emotions and behaviors in challenging times.

insecurities and False information

Doing what is easy can also relate to insecurity. I believe most relationships start off with too many insecurities. When people start relationships without obtaining or giving information about their "lack of"—like where they lack confidence; what their vices' are, shortcomings, doubts, and jealousies are; and what their differences are—they are likely to be doomed or requiring much work. A lot of people don't want to learn or share this information because of fear. Without having the right (truthful) information, with little to no self-awareness, and without being honest with oneself, the difficulties will quickly be revealed, and it will be difficult to conduct a healthy outcome. These types of relationships will end almost every time in disappointment or much worse.

Doing what's easy means most people won't take personal responsibility for their own happiness and well-being. It's much easier to make someone else responsible for our feelings or sense of happiness. The reality is it's not possible to be in a loving or healthy relationship if you don't first know and love yourself. And take responsibility for your happiness and well-being. It's also not reasonable for someone to be responsible for your happiness and overall well-being. We can only hope to have good people contribute to our happiness and well-being (not be responsible).

Doing what is easy means sometimes people gravitate toward mannerisms that bear a strong likeness to what they're used to—such as a certain person in their past. Maybe a woman can see similarities between a man she's dating and her father or a man finds a woman who is like the last girlfriend he once liked. Maybe the person reminds them of someone, and they show their attractive representation of what they're looking for in a mate. Most of the time, people present a superficial image that is very different from who they truly are.

Therefore, it's vital to have truthful and relevant information about the other person, a clear understanding and awareness of yourself, and a set of principles that will tell you what to do and not to do as a person. A healthy relationship cannot be based on just past experiences. If it was that easy it wouldn't be a relationship of the past, they would still be with that person. This is not the easy way, but it's the right way. Focus on true information and understanding how to facilitate a healthy atmosphere and have a clear vision of self-awareness; don't focus on common interests.

So, don't rely on some similarities between one another I like this, and you like this; I like doing this, and you like doing this; and so on. People call these things sharing compatibilities. When we put our attention on sharing some of the same interests and rely on this to sustain our relationships, those relationships will often fail. Many people don't realize that, as we get older, our interests and passion often change.

Similarly, when both partners have a strong physical attraction and there's lots of chemistry in the beginning, people tend to rely on that as their foundation. They don't realize that, as people get older, many times our physical attraction and aggression will change or fade away. This will leave many wondering what happened; after all, we were so compatible in the beginning. This is another way of doing what is easy If we don't get to know and develop ourselves and know the other person, we are just taking that wide and broad road to failure.

Information is the evidence of what is or is not. Sometimes, getting the correct information may not be easy at the beginning of a relationship. But it's always worthwhile and necessary. The more necessary information you gather, the better position you will be in to make the best decision. Obtaining true and relevant information is the key to developing a compatible relationship.

Getting to know someone starts with honest information about what that person believes, their behavior, their principles, and what they stand for as a person. This is what is needed to determine if people's beliefs, behaviors, and attitudes are in alignment with one another to know if you are compatible.

CHAPTER 3

A LETTER OF EXPECTATION

---

a False Hope

I believe many people have false hope when it comes to addressing some of the common questions. These include queries such as, "What's your personality like?" "What things do you like to do?" "What are your sexual desires?" or "Where do you see yourself in the future?" These types of questions don't add up to finding a compatible mate. And many people may not know themselves well enough to truly know the answers. Many believe in finding someone with the same interest and sharing common likes. Even finding a common passion that you share is not enough. You could share the same passion and have opposite core values and be completely opposite when it comes to how you conduct yourself. So, some may look to having a letter of expectation.

When I was young, I strongly believed this was the way to go. I thought, if both partners had a list of expectations that were in synch or agreed to, this would work. I would think of the most important things to me in a partner—including things like having a good attitude toward each other and being willing to take care of each other. The list would also include cooking on a regular, respecting each other, and planning to raise children within the same structures and boundaries. I thought it best I would also make sure I was able to adhere to my potential partner's list of expectations. This would be the foundation on which we'd build.

The problem with having a list of expectations is, as your foundation is it only works when both partners are fulfilling their parts on the list. Remember, in the beginning, you both are liable to say anything to get what you want from the other person.

For example, if a man agrees to the expectations, he may see the benefit if she agrees to give him sex. Or maybe he needs something from her, and he will do what is expected in the beginning to get what he wants. Another example is if a woman agrees to the expectations, she may see it is worth it to follow through perhaps because of her situation or life's conditions at the time to do so. Or maybe she sees some of the good qualities she is attracted to in that man she likes, so why not? Maybe she'll try to meet these expectations and do her best for a while—until she believes the man has truly fallen for her. And then she may relax and be herself. I've been told by many men and have interviewed many more who've said that the woman, after some time, perhaps even years, when she's no longer interested in adhering to these expectations, says, "You need to love me for me," or, "You need to accept me for me" What do you think the man is saying in his mind? Hmm, Let's just say it's a lot more than, "That's not on the list."

Some men expect their partners to remain the same size or very close to it as when they first met. This may be years later after several children working hard to contribute to their cause. This is not a reasonable expectation unless it is her own. Just look at your body now and when you first met her It's called life. If the other person doesn't have those expectations for themselves, how can you? If, when you first met, your partner was not food health conscious or into working out or telling you that these were her desires, why would you expect her size or figure to remain as it was then? As we all know, if a physique-conscious mindset is not a personal desire for either a man or a woman, life happens. In other words, our bodies will change with or without our help.

Fifty-Fifty rule

Many may believe that relationships are based on a fifty-fifty rule. This is another false expectation and unrealistic desire that will lead you down a broken road. If a person expects the other to always pull their 50 percent and when they don't there will be some issues or they won't want to pull their 50 percent, this is a problem. And it goes both ways.

Having expectations for the other person is one of the main causes of stress in life and insecurities in relationships. People usually experience a strong feeling that the other person is trying to change them. This behavior places stress on both partners. Having expectations is the easiest way to find fault in people. The more faults you find in one another, the more quickly you'll lose interest in one another, the less you'll want to spend time together, and the more you'll start to dislike each other and question why you're together!

I have learned by researching many books and studying others that this does not work. Especially in the case when couples stay together for a long relationship, the less you're willing to adhere to any expectations your partner may have. If any expectation doesn't adhere to your own principles or behavior patterns or has importance to you, you most likely won't do it or won't continue to do it over the longer term. Having expectations of each other for the sake of the kids, marriage, or relationship accompanied by the notion that "he should do it if he loves me" or "she should do it for the kids" will lead to the likelihood of unhealthy behavior or being unhappy. The probability is that one or both partners will feel at times that they are carrying the bulk of the weight or engage in behaviors motivated by tit for tat. This will increase and leads to resentment, animosity, and great emotional pain. In addition, the more one or the other feels they tolerate more, the more anger and bitterness will build up inside. This attitude may times leads to depression or violence.

The expectation is a false sense of control and self-gain. When finding or maintaining a union with someone involves a give-and-get mentality, often one partner may feel more give than get. The only time people should have these expectations is when it's commerce based. This mentality should be saved for business and economic transactions, not related to the compatibility of an intimate or personal relationship. Setting expectations for others will always end up in failure.

Basically, any expectations not met and not ongoing will eventually lead to disappointment, hostility, failure, or separation. Don't expect a person to act in a way that they don't already demonstrate. Imagine if people entered relationships with no expectations of the other person; there would be no room for disappointment. What! Many, if not all of us, believe there should be expectations in a meaningful relationship. If the other person is everything you already expect or does everything you believe he or she should, there would be no need for expectations—only the hope that the person remains who he or she is.

People should only have expectations of themselves. Today's culture has a certain outlook because it has conditioned people how to think and has been passed down from generation to generation. There is a fear of not getting hurt and a tendency to put self-gratification first in relationships. And that's what has hurt us all. People were not designed this way. The key is to find a person who meets all your expectations of what you like and need, without trying to meet all your expectations of what you like and need. Or at least the ones that matter most. It's like finding a person who is all of that and that's just who they are. This means finding the person who shares the principles, attitudes, and behaviors that are important to you. No change is needed. A person who values those views and attitudes without doing it *for* you; it's just who they are, a great fit for a relationship. It is just a way of life for that person. We are getting close, just keep reading. I know, we can hardly wait!

CHAPTER 4

WE JUST NEED TO

---

communicate Better

Has anyone heard this before? The idea that we need to communicate better may be the most confusing and misunderstood topic or quality in every type of relationship in the world. Yeah, I said it. Every time there is a problem this is many people's first reference. I say this because most people don't know how to communicate or what it means to have good communication. Yet they say we need to communicate better. Let's go slowly through this chapter and maybe read it twice. I may be on my own with this at first. But give it a chance to settle in and work within you. Also, I recommend reading other books on communication. Understanding the true power of communication will bring you calmness, patience, and the true benefits of listening.

"We just need to communicate better" This may be one of the scariest statements in a relationship. Only because most people don't know what the necessary components are needed to communicate or communicate effectively. Most people believe communication is within the top two most important requirements for a relationship to survive—or so they say! About nine out of ten of every relationship book's biggest focus is on or about communicating well. The books I have read over the past twenty years list communication among the top one or two requirements for a successful relationship. Even if you google relationship advice, you'll find communication in the top three important requirements or qualities of a relationship.

Some people, well most women in relationships, believe they need to know everything—where their partner is going and what he's doing all the time—and they may believe this is a part of good communication. Collecting what, when, where, and how is considered information, rather than communication. Sometimes this is a concerning sign, a sign of controlling behavior, and maybe other underlying insecurities. Some men believe good communication is providing information only on a need-to-know basis and good communication is not arguing. This is another sign of control, fear, and dishonesty and may cover other underlying insecurities.

Effective communication is needed to procure a healthy relationship, I agree. During the many interviews I've had with men and women, both refer to most of the relationship problems being related to lack of communication or miscommunication. He won't talk to me, he won't let me be heard, and he's always lying to me. These are some factors of communication issues but they're more related to a person's character, lack of respect, lack of interest, and both parties having little self-awareness and trust.

How to effectively communicate

Effective communication involves transferring and receiving honest information between one another through verbal, written, and visual aids, including body language. Also, effective communication is understanding what is being transferred by one another and listening carefully, speaking, or writing clearly, and respecting each other's different opinions and information. When practicing communicating, be mindful of your feelings, especially when communicating with your friends and loved ones. Pay attention to the words you say, as well as to your tone, body language, and facial expressions, so it will be easy for the other person to reciprocate. These are all important elements of communicating, as well as being self-aware of your own communication skills.

One important factor in understanding how to effectively communicate is being aware of your own emotions. Effective communication in any relationship doesn't just mean exchanging information. It means being able to control your listening while understanding the information, and the person communicating it. The most important part is knowing how to regulate your responses. This allows the other person to be open.

A healthy conversation involves one person stating a position of concern related to a need, desire, or want in a manner that can be understood by the other person. Both then agree about the concern and respond to what each person wants to do to address the concern and why. Next, they determine together the best way to resolve the concern.

Communicating in relationships deals with the many facets and makeup of each person and his or her experiences. Communication embodies the complete wholeness of the relationship. The exchange in communication encompasses emotions, understanding, expectations, fear, trust, judgment, insecurities, respect, and more. Some communication can take place without anything being said. For example, let's say you're a man and you're brought up to handle certain things while the woman handles certain other things. This could be an understanding based on your background as a form of communication.

Let's look at a specific example. Say you and your partner are driving and the car gets a flat tire. The man would handle that, right? No communication is needed! Some of our communication is very much based on our past experiences, emotions, words, and actions. Not understanding your partner or audience and their experiences can sometimes lead to misunderstandings. Having the appropriate information about your partner, a clear understanding and awareness of yourself, and knowledge of how your emotional responses affect you and the other person will improve your communication.

In addition, not practicing healthy listening will cause your efforts to suffer. "Your success in communicating with a healthy relationship is acting in opposition to how you feel," notes Judge Lynn Toler. By developing a mindset and behavior of what to say and what to do based on what happened, rather responding to the person or what was said to you."

Although communication is very important and facilitates the whole relationship, it is still not the most important quality in a relationship. Yep! I said it. Don't get offended; it's true Let's keep going.

CHAPTER 5

MAKING A RELATIONSHIP WORK

The concept of making a relationship work has been a mystery to me since I was a young adult. I have heard this my entire life. I could never understand the mindset that holds, people can or need to *make* a relationship work; it just doesn't sound right. It sounds too controlling. Ever since I was young, I've believed that a relationship is something a person must want, not need, and should require very little effort. I believe this because there should be so many other things in place out of their control already working on their behalf uniting them together. For example, he behaves the way he should, he thinks like me or the way I need him to, he believes what I believe, and the way he responds to conflict makes me feel so at ease. It's easy breezy and lemon squeezy (sounds like compatibility). But society tells us differently.

I've found no evidence that couples can make relationships work, only that they stay together because of the work. I know; I read many of those books too, and I thought that too. There was a time I went to therapy, the therapist said, "You can make it work." And what the therapists told us was that either she had to, or I had to make it work. One of us had to stop doing this or stop saying that, and I needed to be more like this, or she needs to be more like that. But is that what we want to really make it work? Also, is that the relationship you want?

Now if we carefully examine their definition of "work" regarding marriage or relationship, it sounds like a lot of giving up this and that;

changing this and that; and, yeah, a lot of work! I believe all healthy relationships are about being a good fit; combining both partners' choices in life through principles, attitude, and behavior; and appreciating who the other person is. It's also about two people connecting with beneficial deeds that already exist with one another— because that's just who they are. When a belief system, behavior, and principle fit with the other person, they make a whole assembly (a relationship). It's easy breezy and lemon squeezy (again, I call it compatible) Stay with me.

I have read many books that say when your relationship isn't working, they should do more things together to bring back the spark or interest. That may mean doing things together and spending more time together, even if you don't want to. They should try new things that both may have in common and create new interests. They should practice talking to each other throughout the day without letting a day go by, even if they don't want to. This is something they must be willing to do, even if they don't want to.

People usually go to therapy or counseling to make their relationship work. Maybe some people go to a boot camp for couples for help so they might change their mindset. Some may say taking short or inexpensive trips or vacations may help build back your relationship. Sometimes creating an environment to make them engaged might bring back what is now lost.

I don't know if a person doesn't want to spend time with their partner or believes their partner doesn't want to spend time with them, this makes for a difficult mindset. Yeah, make it make sense. Then, I'm all in Lol.

If those things are not working, others suggest that one of you start making some changes. You see when it comes to relationships, "compromise" is a big word. People like to pull it out of their holsters when things aren't working out the way they want. There could be many things one could do—say, lose your vanity or lose your attitude or maybe it is your criticism you need to let go of or maybe years of bad habits you don't want to give up. Maybe your partner says you're selfish and not compassionate toward his or her feelings.

Maybe you're just a solitude type of person and that's what's causing problems between the two of you. Whatever it may be, many people believe that a successful relationship requires a ton of work and compromise. Just think about what they're saying—you must lose some of yourself, to win us! Most people in society don't spend the time needed to work on themselves. That's why many people see the need to lose yourself to win. Stop!

With much studying, research, and practice, I've determined that true compromise does not make a relationship work! Compromising in your relationship will allow it to survive, not thrive, yes. Who really wants a surviving relationship? No one really wants to be in a relationship that's just surviving, rather than one that is fun, fulfilling, and healthy.

The thing with true compromise is that it won't last. When compromise involves you behaving not like who you truly are or according to what you may believe, chances are, it won't last. A true compromise only has one side winning at a time, while leaving the other person resentful and unsatisfied. You can agree to the compromise, but if you don't feel or think the same about what you are giving up, it will cause strife, even if you continue to do it, year after year.

Making it work will always need compromise, and one partner should never have to ask the other person to give up something of value to them or to change who they are to prove their love.

You both may believe the key to a relationship is to care about the other person's needs and be willing to be humble and give in when compromising. The key is compatibility; if someone believes, behaves, and stands for all the important things you do and likes you for who you are and you think the same about them. The rest is the small stuff, they just fit.

CHAPTER 6

YOU KNOW HOW I AM OR YOU SHOULD KNOW ME BY NOW.

"You should know me by now" is another scary statement someone can make to a loved one in any type of relationship. Many people who have been in a relationship for a while expect their partner to conform to who they are. When one partner says this, he or she is making an arrogant expression of his or her self-importance above all else. This type of attitude and behavior doesn't necessarily mean the person is superior, just that he or she *thinks* of himself or herself as more important in that situation or circumstance. When this behavior becomes frequent, it can become overbearing to deal with in any relationship. An arrogant attitude doesn't mean the arrogant parties are right or never wrong; it just implies they think they are. This type of attitude will affect people's behavior, causing them to act as if they are more important than or know more than their partners or that things should go their way just because. This type of attitude also leaves little room for listening and growing as an individual—which leads arrogant people to share how much they know and has achieved while ignoring others around them.

"You know how I am" can also imply you get what you see, whether right or wrong, good, or bad. Sadly, most people don't show others "how I am" at the beginning of any type of relationship because they themselves know how egotistical this version of themselves can appear. So, most people wait until some time has gone by or the other person is comfortable or has invested time in the relationship to demonstrate this attitude—because they still want results to go in their favor.

This attitude reveals how one chooses to interact with others or not or maybe just with their significant other. It suggests they don't have to fit into any type of expected behavior to be involved with or accepted by others even their significant other. The way they talk or interact will either be understood and accepted or not—because "you know how I am."

The main evidence revealing this type of attitude in a person can be considered self-centered behavior concerned solely with one's own desires, needs, or interests without any outside influences. I'm not including this approach to life as a bad thing or that someone who behaves in this manner is a bad person. I don't suggest this type of behavior to be a healthy trait in a person or for a partner. Such people don't desire to be flexible or to grow. They strongly want the other person to always compromise.

CHAPTER 7

DON'T COMPROMISE, BE COMPATIBLE

Many may believe compromise and communication is the key to the success or failure of a relationship. Many people I've spoken with and many books I have read also say this. This spans all ages and different backgrounds of people over the past thirty years of my encounters. Media has been programming us in thinking communication and compromise solve it all. I believe we may have a clear and false understanding of what position compromise and communication have in facilitating a healthy relationship and have been conditioned to think so throughout this culture.

A compromise is basically a dispute, argument, or difference between two or more people who don't agree on what they want, need, or believe. For example, to truly compromise is to say, I give up something I want, need, or believe, and you give up something you want, need, or believe to meet in the middle, so we compromise. Thus, neither one of us is getting exactly what we want, need, or believe. I know everyone says, in every relationship, you must compromise. I don't believe that a fruitful, fulfilling, and healthy relationship needs compromise. Let's read this chapter again.

Let's say, for example, you and your partner can't decide between Burger King and McDonald's, and one of you guys gives in all the time. I do not consider this a real compromise in the relationship. I call this being reasonable and taking turns choosing where to eat or not sweating the small stuff. No one should always have his or her way or make a big deal about something this small. Stay with me.

True compromise comes into play when something of value disrupts or tears down a relationship. If one of you wants children and one doesn't, this can't be a compromise. If one of you believes in God and one doesn't, this can't be a compromise. If one of you believes child-rearing should be this way and the other one doesn't, this can't be a compromise. This is not a good fit. If one person believes he or she should be the head of the house and the other one doesn't, this can't be a compromise. Anything and everything that is a principle or a set of core values in your life should not be up for compromise. This takes into consideration those things that people justly want, need, or believe to contribute to who they are. The more we compromise who we are or what we value, the more resentful or in a position of servitude we become.

True compatibility is having the same belief system, core values, and alike attitude that results in like behavior. Being compatible means you both believe the same way about what family means, how to raise children, and what core values matter. Being compatible is *not* you both like the same type of movies or going dancing. Being compatible is *not* sharing the same interests and having fun together. You guys just share the same interest and have fun together. Being compatible is not sharing the same passions in life. These things are chemistry and emotionally related connections. Being compatible is having the same belief systems and core principles; respecting and appreciating the other person for who he or she is as a person, separate from you; and basing your respect and appreciation on who your partner is, not who he or she is with you. You like your partner for who he or she is, and your partner likes who you are. You get along well together and benefit one another because of who you are, not because of but despite a situation or circumstance.

When people begin to compromise on things they believe in or their principles to try to make a relationship work, they will only start building bitterness toward their partner. Compromise doesn't work for a healthy relationship, and you shouldn't ask the other person to give up something of value—something that makes that person who he or she is—for you because he or she loves you. Soon your partner will want you to do the same. Where do you think this will lead? Or who will give up first?

CHAPTER 8

LET'S TAKE A BREAK!

You both claim you've done everything. The letter of expectation, making it work, and compromise aren't working. When one or both of you aren't getting what you want or need, then there's talk of, "Let's take a break." When needs are not met and communication and trust aren't working in a relationship, the new now says it's time to take a break. This usually comes up when both partners are doing the same thing and getting the same results, repeatedly. Sometimes people get into a relationship too quickly and clearly don't know themselves or the other person. Moving in too soon is another mistake that may lead to these results. Most of the time, this is a result of ignoring bad behavior or economic conditions. Most habits and patterns are hard to break, and the longer you tolerate them, the harder they are to stop.

If a woman suggests a break, it could mean many things. She may need a break from him. She may need more time to herself, perhaps thinking he'll get his act together. Maybe she wants to test out the waters and so on. She could just want a step back to analyze the relationship to see if she sees a real future with her partner. It could be she wants to see other guys discovering whether the guy she's with really is a great guy or the one for her. Maybe she's lacking excitement in the relationship, and she wants to see if it's her or him. Maybe he's overbearing, and she wants to do some soul-searching to see why she even needs a break in the first place. If a woman wants to take a break it could be any reason.

Now, if a man suggests taking a break, there is a very high chance that he is already done with you or is planning on doing something he wouldn't if he wasn't on a break. In my research, about 90 percent of the time, taking a break is suggested by the woman. Most of the time, the woman thinks her man will get his act together. In my opinion, about 99 percent of the time, that never happens. Let's take a break is not a good idea. It usually doesn't work. Most of the time, this can be avoided if one becomes self-aware, whole, and single first and recognizes how to find a similar type of mate.

If one partner wants the break, make sure that your partner is on board and that the discussion is mutual. If not don't do it! If the break is a break for a healthy reason, be clear. If you're both excited and onboard, there should be some ground rules. Be as clear and honest as possible with the other person about why you both want the break in the relationship. This is vital. If you both can't make sense of the break, don't do it. I still don't believe in breaks!

CHAPTER 9

I THOUGHT WE WERE COMPATIBLE.

I think all people say this in the beginning: It was *great*! We had so much chemistry, we were so connected, we couldn't keep our hands off each other, and we got along so well. This is because it's always good in the beginning for us all. It's good why? We don't know each other yet. It's all chemistry, emotions, hormones, and lust. It is *great*!

In the beginning, mostly we show our good side, our best behavior, and only what we want the other person to see. We say and do whatever it takes to get what we want from the other person. There's no history yet of regretful words and actions, no bad times or struggles, and no knowledge or experience of bad behavior from the other person. The further people get into the relationship without attaining that vital information about each other—which is needed to know—the more likely they will have a failed or unhappy relationship.

Most people find it very important to find a partner who shares similar viewpoints when it comes to sex, music, politics, religion, and family. Most people today will put more concern and importance on their sexual compatibility than important issues, like whether they both want children or how they believe in raising them. Many people's sexual compatibility is more important than how they believe their children should be raised or even what their spiritual convictions and daily lifestyle are.

People in today's culture really get excited when they share similar sexual desires in terms of their turn-ons and turnoffs. Many people in relationships today find that sexual compatibility is in every way more important than many other characteristics in a person. Wow! This is very concerning, I think we all know, or should all know that people's sexual tension, excitement, and attraction will never remain the same, as time and life's experiences catch us!

Sexual desires are at the forefront of most if not all beginning relationships. In our society today, men and women tend to link their sexual interests as part of their compatibility. Many may believe that their sexual connection in relationships is the highest level of connection and attractiveness. They may put too much concern on having that chemistry and physical attraction, believing it to be the foundation of a positive and happy life. Many may fear being with someone with whom they lack that chemistry or have less attraction.

That may be their biggest fear in relationships. The issue is sexual attraction shouldn't be the foundation of a relationship, but a plus, just like sharing a passion. The relationship's foundation should be set on something that won't waver or change, like principles, beliefs, and long-term life habits. There are many books, magazine articles, dating experts, and social media platforms that emphasize the importance of sexual attraction in a relationship—because that's what most people want to hear. For this reason, most people are conditioned to gravitate to this mindset as a foundation or starting point for looking for someone visually and sexually compatible. I'm not mad at you, I want this too, but this mindset results in behaviors that usually lead to having many failed relationships. People set a high priority on their sexual needs, desires, and expectations. Sometimes women use their sexuality as a tool to get what they want or as a weapon to punish their partners because of their partners' behavior. That is dangerous behavior and is not recommended. Because many people put so much importance and attachment on sex, disrespectful and deceitful sexual encounters can become a dangerous and unhealthy pattern of domestic aggression.

This prioritization of sex leads to bad behavior by both the partner who isn't being sexually satisfied and the one withholding. Ultimately this type of behavior leads to a broken and sometimes violent or unhealthy relationship.

In a healthy relationship, sex should be a gift to one another that the other one is always willing to give with no regard. And whenever either partner wants to partake in the gift, they should do so without condition, circumstances, or guilt. Just imagine the ones who are believers in the Faith. If this is your only partner for the rest of their life and they can only be with you, why would you deny them? Think about it. It amazes me that most people don't realize that the role of sex is completely opposite from what they've been led to believe or how it's intended used. In a healthy relationship, sexual satisfaction is elevated when the partners are compatible on all other levels and practicing healthy sexual behavior with one another, each desiring to give to the other; this is where we experience ecstasy. Again, the misunderstanding and misrepresentation about sex are very concerning. We all should know that sexual tension, excitement, and attraction will never remain the same especially if not nurtured. It isn't that sexual attraction and satisfaction need to get worse over time, but reality plays a huge role (time, history, behavior, gravity, health, and so on and so forth)!

Our Creator designed us to be at our best when we commit to one, instead of having multiple partners and multiple experiences with others to protect us from ourselves, especially women. It's our memories He was trying to protect us from primarily. For this reason, people should take picking a partner very seriously and carefully. If a couple is super compatible in their beliefs, attitudes, and behaviors and only has one partner, *wow*! If a couple only has experience with one sexual partner, they won't know when the sex goes bad or how bad the sex is (no disappointment). If they have only one partner, they won't know whether their significant other is up to their sexual expectations (no regret). They will only have that great experience based on the one, however good or great. If both are willing, they only will get better. If people had only one partner, they wouldn't have comparisons or good or bad memories with other partners to consistently focus on. Believe it or not, having the best sexual experience is not found in some super compatible sex partner; this may only give you a great sexual moment. A great sex partner is finding the one with whom you have a great sexual relationship because you're connecting and reconnecting beyond the physical experience. You are able and willing to talk and express yourself sexually openly and truthfully. Therefore, compatibility is so important. Having the right person and the right fit for you will give you the greatest sexual experiences both partners can have.

CHAPTER 10

WE'RE MARRIED NOW!

Women don't get mad. For so many women, once they get married, it becomes the fix-a-man plan. Why? Because we're married now!

Let's break down the fix-a-man plan. I have come to recognize this pattern through discussions with many women over the many years and from what I've seen on TV and other media sources. Many women believe that when they get married—to the man they have been with over time—it's time for him to automatically get it together. I have spoken with many women who have been with their guy for years; all that time, he's had no job and hasn't acted responsibly with money or in his social behavior. Suddenly when they get married, they'll get serious. You need to change—*now*!

Many times, men choose not to mature or take on responsibility in the relationship. This could be the case for many reasons. Sometimes men have a mindset that says, "I'm carefree," helping them release themselves from the responsibilities of life and relationships. If so, don't ignore it. Some men haven't developed their independence because of their past and still need to be taken care of. We're married now, won't fix this.

Having reasonable balance when it comes to a partner's behavior is crucial to fulfilling a healthy relationship. If you are with a man or woman for a long period of time and he or she displays a certain behavior or conducts him or herself in a certain way, you should accept that. If you don't accept the way he or she addresses life, you will invite opportunities for stress, arguing, disagreements, and more.

Sometimes, a man will be completely upfront and honest with a woman and tell her, "This is who I am." Most of the time, a woman will not accept the truth and reality of a man who clearly demonstrates who he is because—we're married now, and you need to change. What?

There are times when people expect their spouses to fulfill most of their emotional and companionship needs and to become the primary source of their happiness. Some people also believe they should be their spouse's center of attention most of the time. The frightening one is when some couples believe the excitement and passion should continue as it was earlier in the relationship for the duration. Those of us who have been in this rodeo for a while know the intensity and reality of these expectations are unrealistic at best. I'm sorry for the newbies, but it's good you found out now.

There are a few things that should be predictable or normal in relationships or marriages. These include commitment, trust, respect, and healthy communication. I don't believe in making a relationship or marriage work, just like I don't believe we're married now, will fix anything.

If people rely on sex or intimacy for the relationship or marriage based on, what we married now should expect discomfort, challenges, and hardship in their relationship. Intimacy will always change and fluctuate. Passion can come and go depending on many factors surrounding how we feel. And our commitment doesn't rely on either one of these factors. This is because these two can waver and commitment should be connected to our beliefs and principles part of us that shouldn't waver.

As I mentioned before, being compatible means, you fit well together without having to work at being together and appreciate, respect, and enjoy each other. It's easy. Compatibility is the natural alignment of your life choices and values with the other person's life choices and values. Compatibility has nothing to do with love or interest, because love is a choice, and interest can often change. Compatibility (core life choices and core values) should never change. If you believe you are compatible with someone, you should hope that nothing about who he or she is as a person will ever change. A person cannot become compatible with someone before becoming self-aware first.

CHAPTER 11

WHERE DO I BEGIN?

Self-aware

Most couples look for that glue in the other person to hold them together during times of stress and difficulties. Most couples look for or expect their partners to bridge the gap for them, fill in their insecurities, or be their better half. People are shown and, many times told that, without these types of relationships, we would have a sedated, numb, or dead spirit inside of us; or maybe we would have a lack of connection to our true selves. We are taught at such an early age to depend on relationships and other people. We're told that a partner will increase our value or overall well-being. But this is not true. Many relationships can help or hurt us. Our overall well-being is maintained through God, self-appreciation, and self-application.

Men and women need different things for different reasons in a relationship—just as daughters have different needs from fathers than do sons and sons have different needs from mothers than do daughters. Throughout our lives, we're taught the need to belong to someone is necessary to become whole (not true).

From childhood to adulthood, we're taught by society through media and consciously, as well as subconsciously conditioning that relating to others and belonging in a relationship is of utmost importance. Rather, the whole time, we were designed by our Creator to only belong to Him and not even to ourselves. People are intended to manage themselves through our natural design. This is because, without God, we don't know how abundantly we are to treat ourselves or others. The only other time you don't belong to yourself is when you get married. Then you belong to God and your spouse (See *The Perfect Marriage* and *Marriage Released* by Darrell Canty, soon to be published)

Become Self-aware

We can find many platforms everywhere to show and teach us how to treat ourselves to be healthy, physically. Many people of all backgrounds have not been taught or shown how to treat themselves in healthy ways spiritually, emotionally, or psychologically. Rather, the emphasis is placed on the importance of treating others well or looking to others to meet their needs. Almost no one is taught true self-development in these areas throughout life. Sometimes we see this lightly verbalized in self-help environments, but it's not backed by many actions or practice. Many times, we can only find this type of help, training, or demonstrations threw professional help. Basically, we were never taught to be self-aware and to have a self-concept that develops self-worth, creating a godlike self-image. But, in truth, our Creator designed us in His image to be like Him (to think, emote, and engage in a divine way).

Being self-aware and cultivating awareness, both consciously and subconsciously, of your principles and your emotional state regularly promotes growth. I believe most of the world's population is unaware of being self-aware. Why? Because in most cultures, we are never taught self-awareness and self-love to keep the masses weak.

Most cultures focus on materialistic needs and self-preservation as most important and most necessary, placing little to no attention on self-awareness or self-development. Self-awareness is a practiced behavior and needs purposeful cultivation to achieve full clarity.

When you consciously practice self-awareness, you will evaluate your principles and emotional conditions in your daily interactions in life. For example, you learn to pay attention to the way you feel, think, and behave in any challenging or difficult situation or argument. The more you evaluate your principles and emotions while considering any challenging situations and questioning your decisions based on your principles, to better your personality, and the better individual you'll become. The more you practice the more you become what your choices reveal. You should focus on becoming self-aware of your emotional conditioning carefully. People can't always choose how they feel or their emotional disposition. Because the way people respond emotionally is a choice, not the cause of a reaction based on an action. That's a behavior. Managing your behavior and having controlled responses to your emotions will take practice. With practice, no one can invoke or control your emotional output. You may not be able to control how you feel, but you can always control how you respond.

The ability to become self-aware is one of the most difficult and most important achievements in life. Self-awareness is a learned skill that anyone can master. To improve his or her character and behavior; with the right exercises and by forming the right habits, clear self-awareness can be achieved by anyone. Developing these habits will help you understand and improve your personality and strengthen your character.

Let's look at some of the behaviors that will help you develop and increase self-awareness. For one, pay attention to things that bother you about other people. Be aware of the way you think, feel, and behave when something bothers you and why it bothers you. This means understanding what happened and how you explained it to yourself to make sense of how you responded (thought, felt, and behaved).

To cultivate this behavior, the first step is to stop; don't respond; and think about the situation, not the person behind it. That way, you won't escalate how you feel. Next, meditate in your mind on all that is involved to identify how you *should* behave according to the situation to achieve the best outcome.

Always reflect on your thoughts, moods, and behaviors related to each incident you're experiencing good and bad, and give yourself feedback. The challenges and problems we face most times seem bigger than they really are because we're in the heat of the moment. Sometimes we blow things out of proportion, or they may seem distorted. Therefore, it's good to give yourself feedback to get clarity and view a given situation from a different perspective. It's good to identify your emotional weakness to learn skills to improve them. If we pay attention to how we act and behave in certain situations and identify our default responses, we can change them, developing new habits and tendencies.

Don't repeat what's not working. Not only will cultivating new and improved actions enable us to develop better relationships because we will be more self-aware, but it will also improve our mood; how we behave and feel in certain situations; and, ultimately, our attitude. Self-awareness also makes for clearer thinking and better decision-making because we are not thinking based on our emotions.

Another habit to develop is the acceptance of constructive criticism. You can practice criticizing yourself and taking criticism from others. This is about building your confidence in yourself and becoming the least defensive you possibly can. The more you practice this, the more you will be able to minimize your reactions to life's situations and recognize the small stuff. We all have flaws. But to embrace yours, you must first know them. This means you need to be open and willing to accept them. You must avoid being defensive at all costs to grow and improve your flaws. You don't need to feel good about your flaws; just know you can do something about them. The less defensive you are, the less impact it will have on you and on others. Being self-aware allows you to plan the outcome of how you behave in any situation before the situation ever occurs.

For example, let's say you're a person who doesn't like wasting time and believes everything should be done in a timely fashion. Being self-aware when you are in a situation where you are visiting or on someone else's time schedule is important. Let's say the person you're visiting typically takes three hours for dinnertime, while your dinnertimes usually take half an hour. You can choose to have a different perspective and attitude while you are there. You can prepare ahead of time, so the prolonged dinnertime won't bother you. And you can understand that you have no control over the situation. Or maybe you can plan a different approach to dinner.

Becoming self-aware will provoke you to become more proactive and more accepting and encourage self-development. Starting these practices will allow you to develop self-control and to practice better decision-making. Self-awareness is based on awareness between thought, emotion, and behavior and what we believe, want, or need. This will invoke more effective communication and interaction with yourself and others.

the Five Key components

Practicing self-awareness behaviors provides you ownership of your emotions, a clear view of yourself and your self-concept, and the ability to assess your strengths and weakness—all while building confidence and executing behaviors to produce specific results. Below is a list of five key components that comprise the skill set and resource of self-awareness:

- Identifying emotions
- Identifying self-perception
- Identifying strengths and weaknesses
- Developing strong self-confidence
- Implementing self-efficacy

Identifying Emotions

Identifying your emotions can be a strenuous process while paying attention to what bothers you about other people and certain situations. Relationships are based on awareness between thought, emotion, and behavior and what you believe, want, or need. This will invoke more effective communication and interaction with another person. Identifying and understanding your emotions and moods when you tend to act or behave in certain ways in response to certain situations, especially those that are difficult or uncomfortable, is crucial. It means paying attention to your default responses to things and why you may feel or act that way. It also means paying attention to and trying to learn about your own psychology. The more you practice doing this, the more aware you'll become.

A benefit of self-awareness includes becoming clear about what we want and need and the level of importance each of those desires and needs truly holds—which may not always match the way we see their importance without the benefit of awareness. As we become more aware of ourselves, we feel less and less compelled to defend our interactions with others. This becomes easier because our mood should improve as we come to feel better about our behavior—chosen actions, rather than reactions. The more we improve our awareness between thoughts, emotions, and behavior, the easier it will be to regulate our feeling and moods.

Identifying Self-Perception

Identifying self-perception leads to clearer thinking and better decision-making. Many times, poor decisions come from disarrayed thinking and a strong emotional reaction. When we become more aware of our habits and how we think and feel, we will experience fewer short-term impulses and take more actions based on long-term values and netting healthier results. With self-perception comes a clear sense of decision-making that doesn't respond to just right now. Self-perception is all attitude on how you see your behavior or others.

Identifying Strengths and Weaknesses

Self-perception leads to identifying and assessing your strengths and weaknesses. To assess your strengths and weaknesses, you must be realistic and optimistic. You must pay attention and develop a sensible idea of what can be achieved or expected in a disagreement or during a difficult or uncomfortable situation. This course of action must be practiced as often as recognized. The practice of identifying your strengths and weaknesses will help you become someone who has a good grip on the reality of a situation and understands what can or can't be done.

There isn't always a right or wrong outcome. Self-perception, most times, will expose a practical, achievable idea or reveal something that resembles the truth about the situation and sometimes not the person or vice versa.

This behavior also allows you not to always judge the people involved in a situation and, rather, focus on the issue. Self-perception creates more effective communication, making it easier to communicate confidently but not assertively. The better we know ourselves, our strengths, and our weaknesses, the better approach we can take and the more productive we can be in effectively communicating and relating to others.

Having a good attitude about bettering oneself is empowering and a foundation for healthy relationships. I believe a good attitude derives from good thoughts, which come from a positive belief system and the understanding that it's not about control and, rather, about management. I say this because, if we focus on our attitude and never on the problem, we'll improve how we deal with each problem. An opportunity and situation—regardless of little control we may have or not was once a possibility of a problem. We can focus on knowing that we can't control a situation or a person, but we can always control ourselves and our response to the person and/or situation.

Identifying Self-Confidence

Having a good attitude will help you develop strong self-confidence and the ability to manage your thoughts, emotions, and behavior. A position of constant self-awareness can help eliminate many hidden obstacles and increase your strategies for becoming better at dealing with life's challenges. Sometimes the things that irritate us in other people may reflect some quality we dislike in ourselves.

One way to develop good self-confidence is to read high-quality nonfiction. That's right. Read some self-help books. Most great readers, writers and creators are very good observers of the world around them. Also, pay attention to the little details and functions of life. Learn how to describe people carefully and how to think about people with compassion. This will build your confidence. The better we get at observing others, the better we will get at observing ourselves in the same way.

Developing strong self-confidence starts with identifying what things trigger your emotional "red button." Maybe it's more than one button. We all have certain emotions that trigger us. Most people try to avoid feeling these emotions by substituting other emotions or behavior that may lead to negative consequences in the long term. We must not try to avoid our emotions when they affect us in a negative way but, try to listen to what our emotion has to say. The first step in cultivating a system to think developmentally is to come from a foundation of self-awareness. Create new habits.

The best approach in every situation is don't respond right away. First, be calm and think. Is it the person or situation? And then reflect on your ability to choose your emotion and not let your emotion choose you (don't respond right away). Developing a strong self-confidence leads to becoming a good validator (that's another book).

Implementing Self-Efficacy

Implementing self-efficacy begins with deliberately and carefully considering your weaknesses and aspiring to your strengths. It means developing your capacity to execute new behaviors and perform better with practice. Basically, plan and work it. You can practice this behavior by choosing a positive relationship in your life, like a relationship with a friend, spouse, parent, or someone else close to you. Start with some small things the other person can offer you criticism of; ask them to point out something negative to help build their confidence that you can take criticism well. Start working on those issues with feedback and work on the approach technique I noted earlier. The more you practice reflecting on your shortcomings, the more you will build up the other person's confidence that you can take criticism. And they will be more likely to tell you about more major personality issues if there are any. Try to avoid defensiveness and anticipate that you won't feel good about your flaws, but these exercises will help eliminate them. To get better with any problem, you must first find out what the problem is.

Make a daily journal of your encounters throughout the day and how you handled each one. Look at each interaction and categorize it to see if your behavior is different depending on if you're at work or with a friend. Constantly reflect on your views and choices and each reaction to challenging situations. Go back and review the self-awareness sections for tips. For more details or problematic issues on implementing these five key components, please seek professional help.

CHAPTER 12

BECOMING A WHOLE PERSON

Self-Love

If you're not whole and you believe you have found a whole person, he or she will need to take from themselves in the areas you are not whole to make you whole. When this happens, the person who has taken from him or herself to make you whole will no longer be whole. This doesn't mean you are not supposed to contribute to each other and help one another grow. If you both are whole, whatever you give to the other is overflow; whatever is given isn't making the person whole but, rather, better.

Becoming a whole person involves utilizing our mind, will, emotion, and body to operate in an integrated and holistic manner. It's using all these elements together to make the whole greater than the entirety of its parts. This is how our Creator intended us to be. Therefore, as we practice carefully and consciously what we feed each part, we develop a subconscious foundation of mental, emotional, and spiritual principles.

This may be one of the most enlightening chapters of the books for many people. Personal development to become a whole person is making a commitment and an ongoing investment in yourself, so you can become the best version of yourself.

With commitment and the right discipline, your efforts in self-improvement and becoming self-aware will be amazingly positive and rewarding.

Your relationship with God and with yourself should be the most important thing in your life. This is the key to a healthy relationship with any person. The greatest commandment ever given by Jesus was based on self-love.

the Greatest Commandment

"One of the teachers of the law came and heard them debating Noticing that Jesus had given them a good answer. Of all the commandments, which is the most important? The most important one answered Jesus, is this: Hear, O Israel: The Lord our God, the Lord is Love, Lord your God with all your heart and with all your soul and with all your mind and with all your strength. The second is this: Love your neighbor as yourself. There is no commandment greater than these."

After completely assessing your strengths and weakness and consistently practicing your self-awareness components to become a better you, these are tools you will use to develop your wholeness.

As a whole person and joining with a whole person, you should never think or feel your relationship requires work. I know most people and most books say the opposite. They all claim that every relationship takes work, and most relationships today do require work. This is true with most relationships today because neither partner is whole. If we all continually work on ourselves, the relationship no work! No worries!

Before you reach the highest level of self-love and completely love yourself, you must understand wholeness. You must know the areas of development to focus on, which are spiritual, emotional, social, psychological, physical, and financial. Focusing and developing on these six areas of growth will allow you to live a balanced and rewarding life.

CHAPTER 13

THE SIX AREAS OF GROWTH

You don't necessarily need to focus on developing these six areas of growth in the order listed. But I recommend you attend to spiritual growth first because I believe the spiritual foundation is the core element of every person's center foundation (See my upcoming book *How to Develop Spiritually to Connect to You* by Darrell Canty).

Now, let's look at each of the six areas of growth:

1. *Spiritual-* Spirituality is the essential piece of the whole person. Without a clear understanding of your spiritual awareness and authority, you will gravitate to your basic need of self-preservation and physical security, and that will take priority in your focus. Connecting to your spirituality means finding your basic purpose and linking it to yourself and how you spiritually see the world around you. Your spirituality is governed by your natural aspect of goodness, passion, and greed. And this is how you will develop your social connection to naturally drive the beliefs, views, and choices that form and develop your personality. You will cultivate within yourself behavior that reveals your character, functioning from a foundation of optimism, compassion, and reality. Regardless of your faith, religion, or belief system, developing your spirituality will guide and promote your relationships.

2. *Emotional-* Your emotional intelligence or lack thereof will shape who you are. Your emotions affect your thoughts,

behavior, and beliefs and how you react to people and situations in life. Your emotional awareness determines your ability to handle situations and how you see yourself and others. Your spiritual and emotional Intelligence are the most important elements of your wholeness because they have the most effect on your *human-being* and outcome in life. Emotional intelligence creates leadership skills, social skills, and self-help skills. Your emotions affect every area of your life.

3. *Social-* Social involvement comes into play in almost everything we do in life. Understanding how to form and maintain good relationships with others depends highly on your spiritual and emotional awareness and your connection with yourself (self-love). Your success in acting and interacting properly in different social environments very much depends on how well you develop your emotional intelligence and emotional control through self-love.

4. *Psychological-* Psychological growth is basically dealing with and developing your mind and emotional state. It also involves elevating your awareness to influence, motivate, or engage with intellectual or emotional concepts with others. The psychological aspect of a whole person relates to the understanding of one's true inner self, self-esteem, self-concept, and self-acceptance. The most important relationship you'll ever have is any relationship is the one you have with yourself. If you like and believe in yourself, it's easier for everyone else to like and believe in you too.

5. *Physical-* Physical health represents your total well-being and the key to your existence on earth. *With-no-body there is no you.* Physical health incorporates adequate sleep, healthy food, hygiene, activity, and relaxation. I advise every person to take his or her physical health seriously because it affects your mental and emotional well-being. Your good physical health

prevents disease and improves how you feel. Good physical health is good for maintaining energy to push through the day and provides confidence in all areas of life, including work, parenting, activities, and social relationships. Good health is the foundation of a good attitude.

6. *Financial* I believe people spend too much time on financial and professional aspirations. I believe if you spend more time developing the other five elements of a whole person, this one will fall into place. The financial arena is usually the greatest producer of stress, problems, and issues in people's lives. And we spend the most time on our finances. Society puts so much pressure on working and making money that it oftentimes prevents people from seeing themselves. I'm going to keep it short; if you get the other five, you will have a good attitude and be in control of your mind, body, and emotions—which will make it much easier to get your finances in order. The other five help make a better person; finances will only make better situations.

To develop each area of your wholeness to become a whole person, start with making a list of your strengths and weaknesses. This process will require a great deal of discipline and time and constant reflection on both your strengths and weaknesses. You need to set daily, weekly, and monthly goals for each area of your life. Make sure that, when you set your goals, they are simple and realistic. It's not going to be easy to apply this kind of discipline and balance to real-life situations.

By engaging daily in personal development, you can develop your strategic and creative thinking, listening, speaking, problem-solving, and coaching. Think about each of the aspects of the areas of growth and see how they relate spiritually, mentally, and emotionally. With the right knowledge and behavior, you will become more confident, fulfilled, and empowered in every area of your life.

CHAPTER 14

BE SINGLE FIRST

Being self-aware, whole, and single first assure the success of a healthy, happy, and intimate relationship with self-first and a worthy life. As Dr Myles Munroe, a Bahamian author, speaker, and leadership consultant wisely notes, "Singleness is the most important state of human development, and it is the foundation of God's design for the human family."

In truth, most people aren't given at a young age the direction or taught how to be self-aware and develop into a whole person. In truth, most people don't know or value their self-worth or the self-worth of others. In truth, most people engage in relationships based on assumptions, their needs, and possibilities of self-gratification. In truth, about half of all the homes in America are and have been without a father for many years, which usually has a negative impact on how people think, grow, and behave. In truth, most people don't know how to be single.

Being effectively single is first knowing who you are; it's being whole and ready to equip yourself with life's tools to be independent, resilient, and practical when facing life's challenges. Practice and develop your ability to manage your time between work, friends, and specific activities. Learn how to prioritize and simplify with the things that matter most in your life. Practice identifying and eliminating distractions so you can maximize opportunities and make the best use of time. Try not to pick up on many vices that require much time, money, and bad habits. Establish routines that strengthen and build and reveal healthy behavior. Most importantly, manage your relationships and money carefully and consciously because these two can be the most dangerous or rewarding to your whole situation. To do these things is to be effectively single; it's not searching for someone to help you out when you are lacking so much of a whole you.

The objective of being successfully single is to establish a solid intrapersonal relationship with yourself. You will become effective at assessing your situation or circumstance to develop a strong self-concept and self-image. You'll be able to clearly understand your own thoughts and feelings, all while analyzing a situation clearly, being objective and reflective. Developing a healthy intrapersonal relationship promotes self-love and understanding, self-acceptance, and appreciation— enough to share yourself.

The first gift God gave to humanity is His Image. His image means thinking and emoting with free will. Being single is taking the time to strengthen your self-image. Having a positive and firm concept of yourself is empowering and necessary. Do things to protect your memory of you. Do things to take care of yourself mentally, practice emotional management, and improve your physical abilities. Also, do things you enjoy and spend time with people who are whole and self-aware. All these things demonstrate self-love. Don't waste time with people who constantly take from you or bring you down, because they are not whole or helpful.

Develop your spiritual presence and self-confidence until there is no need for someone else to encourage, motivate, or compliment you to be you or feel good about yourself. Single is the time to learn life's lessons and build your experiences and personality. While you are single, you need to learn to cultivate yourself and others.

To cultivate is to improve or make better. You need to be able to continually improve yourself and your environment. Until you become secure and self-assured enough in your own individuality to function properly in any situation, stay single. Be aware enough to determine whether people enjoy being around you because you can improve the environment.

Being effectively single is functioning and operating without depending on other people's approval or resources to make a living. You should take at least a year to be on your own and single before you engage in any relationship—at least a year.

Being single is for mastering your awareness of how to control your words in challenging situations. It's having the ability to safeguard your own, your friends and your loved ones' confidence, trust, and dignity.

You know you are ready for a relationship or marriage when you don't need to be in one and when you are comfortable spending time with yourself, alone. One of the keys to finding a good mate is being a good mate.

OK, you say you're ready. Now that you're self-aware, whole, and successfully single and feeling empowered and complete, what are the few things you need to know to have a healthy, fulfilling, and fruitful relationship? You are clearly on the narrow road that will lead you there, but let's make sure you have all the tools needed to get you through.

There are many qualities people believe are necessary to sustain a relationship. This is a *must*, there are six. The tools you need on your relationship journey are honesty, respect, trust, communication, forgiveness, and intimacy.

CHAPTER 15

THE SIX QUALITIES FOR

Building a Relationship

Honesty

As I've mentioned, I've been seeking to understand relationships for the past twenty-plus years, primarily relationships between men and women. The search has been fueled by an ongoing hunger to find the correct answers to get the best outcome.

I've interviewed hundreds of men and women and asked the question, "What is the most importation quality in a relationship?" And surely and sadly, almost all of them said communication or compromise. Less than 1 percent chose a different quality, and only a handful said honesty. Most of the books I have read conclude that communication and compromise are the most important qualities in a relationship. Frightening, yes. It's frightening that media and society have influenced or manipulated most people's beliefs and understanding of what's truly important in a relationship without seeing the reality. Hopefully, you can carefully review what I revealed, as it's different than what we've all been told. Don't go anywhere.

Honesty is the most important quality in any person and any relationship. Honesty is the seed that grows our character. Honesty with yourself and others leads to a fullness of life. It's not just about telling the truth It's about being real with yourself and others about who you are, what you want and need, and how you live.

Honesty also influences and promotes openness, accountability, and self-control. Honesty represents the entirety of integrity; it means living upright' being truthful, sincere, responsible, and loyal; and using good judgment. Honesty is essential to the whole relationship and facilitates all the other qualities in a relationship. If you took honesty out of the relationship, what other quality would matter?

I believe that, while the other qualities of a good relationship—communication, trust, respect, forgiveness, and intimacy—are important, honesty is the actual glue between you and your partner. When you lose that glue, you will eventually fall apart.

I know I know; I didn't mention love with the other elements. I will explain and cover the subject of love toward the end of the book.

Stay with me

Why do I say honesty is the glue for all the other qualities?

- *Honest communication* connects people to what they need. Any form of communication is about connecting, understanding, and achieving your purposes. Let's say your partner is communicating, but the information is not true or is deceitful. How valuable is that communication to you? False communication won't achieve your purpose.

- *Honest trust* builds. In other words, honesty builds trust. Trust has no foundation without honesty. People are comfortable and willing when they know the other person cares enough to tell the truth.

- *Honest respect* originates from admiration. People admire those who show integrity and an attitude of consideration. Basically, to respect someone, you must favor or like them; it's very easy to like and respect honest people.

- *Honest forgiveness* is truly caring about someone. When someone is not honest with you, forgiveness is almost impossible, as that person may believe their health, welfare, or security is not important to you. They don't know! They don't care!

- *Honest intimacy* is purely based on trust and treatment. As we just discussed, honesty builds trust. Without trust, the treatment isn't real, so there is no intimacy. Intimacy is a closeness between people in a personal relationship, and it's hard to be intimate with someone you don't trust—someone who isn't honest.

communication

Communication is the aspect of relationships most talked about. I believe this word is so important because most people believe communication is the most important thing in a relationship. And because most relationship books are written and read by women, it makes it easy to lose its true value. Respectfully, let's go through this section with a lot of care. Most self-help books related to money, finance, or profession are read mostly by men. So, my guess is about 80 percent of readers are women when it relates to relationships. Does that mean writers need to give the readers (women) something they want to read? Yes! What do women want? Communication, compromise, if you love me; you will change for me; or how to make this relationship work; and so on. Communication in a healthy relationship starts with being honest and open to sharing information with a clear understanding. Many times, people in a personal relationship don't know how to share their feelings while communicating in a clear way. We can discover this later (See my upcoming book *How to Speak Clearly… and How to Get What You Want From A Man.*

As I mentioned, honesty is the most important element in communicating. Great communication includes being respectful and patient. Good communication is having the ability to let things go when time and behavior have demonstrated it's time to do so. I am grateful if you are a woman and reading this book; thank you, I am grateful because you are mostly the ones seeking better and healthy relationships for many communities out there, and many times you are the problems. Most men just aren't that interested. I'd rather share something that can really help you and your partner in a relationship than give you something you just want to read, like *Act Like a Lady, Think Like a Man* Don't Tell Steve Lol.

All relationships are important, and with great communication skills, both people can feel appreciated and accepted and will thrive. When communication is good and healthy, it helps avoid misunderstanding, attitude, and resentment. When good communication is present, it can improve a person's mood and productivity.

I've also experienced the power and destruction of using negative words. Always try to use positive words—even when you're trying to express some of your negative feelings. It will increase respect and intimacy. Communicate, communicate, communicate. Remember, in the beginning, the less you communicate, the worse it will get. But later in the relationship the less you communicate the better it can get. Women be sweet like sugar, to make it easy for men to talk to you. It's hard to communicate with anyone when the other person is angry, moody, unpleasant, loud, and disrespectful and you can't be heard.

trust

I've been told and have heard most of my life that trust can be earned. I have tested this theory myself after studying many other people's stories over the years and found this not to be true. Trust is the firm belief in the reliability of a person or thing. Trust in a relationship is usually a verbal and nonverbal agreement of belief, behavior, and in responsibilities. Trust is also confidence in the honesty or integrity of a person or thing. When couples are in a personal or intimate relationship, they trust in the other enough to be comfortable confiding in him or her because they feel safe and secure with that person. Trust in a relationship is having faith in someone to be loyal to you and to love you. Trust is given based on the integrity of a person or a thing and cannot be earned based on the merit of something comparable, Trust me!

There are some signs when you can trust people. One is when they keep their conversations and actions open and transparent. Another is when they share deep secrets and fears about themselves. When this happens, you should reciprocate. Trustworthy people always admit to their mistakes and share needed information with you. I believe trustworthy people are active listeners who show they care for you and respect your feeling enough for you to trust them.

Being able to trust your partner is essential, especially during the difficult times. Losing trust in the groundwork causes people to fail in their relationships. Love and intimacy in a relationship can't exist without trust. People truly rely on those whom they trust, which involves trusting them to do the things they've promised to do. Trust goes far beyond trusting your partner not to cheat on you; it's about knowing that your partner has your back no matter what and regards your emotional and mental state highly and with care.

Trust helps people overcome obstacles. No matter what you're up against, you know deep down you feel safe and secure with your partner. Trusting also is a key element in healing. You trust that your partner really cares for you, despite the issues the two of you face. Trust gives you the reassurance that your partner wants, appreciates, and loves you despite the situation. Real trust is when you don't need to justify your actions because your partner knows you by your principles and your behavior.

respect

Respect is my favorite quality. I believe respect is or should be the most appreciated quality in any relationship because one must like a person to respect him or her.

Other than professional relationships, respect is given, not earned. To respect someone is to treat or think of that person with kindness, care, and concern. People who respect someone listen to them and give them the courtesy of truly hearing what's being said. Respectful people are thoughtful of others' feelings and acknowledge them with patience and kindness.

Being respectful is acknowledging when other people are respectful and considerate and usually have a habit of being thankful. Respectful people respect physical and emotional boundaries according to each person's preferences.

Some forms of respect are defined a little differently from a man's perspective than from that of a woman. For example, let's say the two of you are out at the grocery store and you run into an old friend, for most women, it's a must—a sign of respect—that you introduce her to the friend. It doesn't matter if it is a guy or a girl. Most women want to know all the people you know when you are in a relationship. Also, most women want you to acknowledge them to others in any situation. Here's another example, the two of you are out at a bar or the movies, and you run into one of your exes; it's a must that you look and act excited to be with your girl, and it's a must that you introduce her as your girlfriend, fiancée, wife, or whatever her title is or should be. Doing so is one of the highest ways to show respect to a woman.

Let's look at another example. When you guys commit, you must tell her about every necessary woman in your past with whom you had a serious relationship; not doing so could cause any future problems. Also, men you should have no serious secrets that affect her emotionally; that's respecting her. All these are examples of respect if you execute correctly or disrespect if you don't.

Respect for a man mostly relates to how a woman carries herself—how she looks, dresses, and acts, regardless of whether her man is with her or not. For example, even when a man met a woman who later becomes his significant other, she was looking, dressing, or acting less than ladylike, but now that they're a couple. He'll expect his woman to look, dress, and act in a certain way, regardless of how they met. It's like the woman who met a man without a job who couldn't keep a job and didn't want a job and then says, "We're married, now, Get a job!"

Another example, of the highest respect a woman can show to a man, involves how she speaks to him and others. Whether he's sixteen or sixty-six, no man wants a woman speaking to him loudly, disrespectfully, and out of control.

Forgiveness

This extremely valuable quality of forgiveness is often overlooked as not being very important. I believe giving and forgiving are the two most valuable riches and rewarding experiences in life for people. If you acquire all the other qualities in life but can't forgive people, this quality will contaminate all the others. Try it. Forgiving someone is purely for the benefit of you, the forgiver. When you forgive someone, it releases you from the stress, worry, tension, and animosity of trying to deal with the person involved in the situation or understand why it happened. When you sincerely forgive someone, let it go, so you don't have to deal with the daily pressures of how you felt before you chose forgiveness. Again, let it go. To forgive is to let go, not forget. When you let go of something, it no longer belongs to you, and it won't affect you as a constant burden. If you are with someone and you can't let it go, let them go. Unforgiveness will eat a person alive.

intimacy

When two whole people link in intimacy, it's about putting the other person's cares, health, feelings, and welfare first. Intimacy at its height is mostly more than the physical part. One of the biggest misconceptions of intimacy is self-gratification. Intimacy first starts with willingness and desire to satisfy the other because of how it pleases you. Intimacy is the ability to share moments of giving, getting, and expressing all that feels good emotionally and physically. It's connecting, together with strong chemistry and attraction. You and your partner share together as a unit—each sharing all of who you are and truly accepting your own and each other's physical and emotional needs in fullness.

If you are not whole, get whole. Or you will continually have struggles with yourself and your partner, and your partner, with you. Fulfilled intimacy is nearly impossible if you have insecurities and fear of any kind within yourself. You must go back to the self-awareness section and discover what insecurities you have and work them out, to be fully intimate with yourself or anyone.

I believe to be a soul mate is to connect two mindsets, two desires of the will, emotionally while aligning ideas, opinions, and awareness of each other's pleasures. I believe two people can experience a blissful intimacy with one another that surpasses just the physical and emotional. When two people get together and choose to connect in all areas—spiritual, emotional, social, psychological, physical, and financial—through life, it's easy to unite as soulmates and experience this blissful intimacy; there are no issues. Connecting yourself with them—with you giving fully and them giving fully— surpasses the emotional feeling and is a truly heavenly experience.

CHAPTER 16

BE A COMPLETE PERSON

Love First

First, I'd like to speak a little about love and family before we get into the interview. Most people have their own version or understanding of love. This could be because of the highly diverse arrangements of family and people's individual outlooks in society. Maybe it's because of the media's projection that there is no norm; there are just different characters with people accepting each person's own identity and behavior in society. I believe that today, there is no societal agreement or understanding on attributes considered to be average or the norm, and sometimes what is clearly right or wrong.

This is primarily due to people's acceptance of the new "you be you," or "you do you." This type of approach leaves little clarity or accountability for a person's actions and belief system. You are probably wondering, *what does this have to do with love?* I believe the key to a healthy and fulfilled you and a healthy and fulfilled life, as well as a healthy and fulfilled society is the correct perspective of self-love and love itself.

In addition, we've been confused or even mislead by the broad definition of what love is or what it represents. Maybe we need to choose our words more carefully when communicating love to one another. Or maybe we need to understand the true concept behind love. We say we love our dog, we love our car, we love basketball, we love seafood, and on and on. Many times, we add the time, energy, and effort behind these things that equal the same value and make it hard for even ourselves to differentiate.

Love is an action word, a word of service and servitude. Love is a choice, not a feeling. It may demonstrate and reveal feelings, but it is not a feeling. True love is given with the hope of reciprocation, not expectation. Just as you should love yourself even when you don't want to, love is showing kindness even when the person you are kind to is not kind to you. Love is demonstrating to the other person to show you are for them without benefits to you. Love is forgiving someone who hurt you and doesn't deserve it. Love is patience—having the capacity to accept trouble, delay, and suffering not in your control without getting upset. Love is sympathy for someone; it's feeling bad or showing sorrow for someone else's misfortune. Love is seeing a need for someone and doing something to avoid damage or risk to their health and welfare. Love is accepting someone for who they are and not who you want them to be. And self-love is to ensure these things for yourself.

Again, the greatest commandment ever given to man by Jesus was based on self-love. There are a hundred Bible verses that talk about loving thy neighbor as thy self.

Even if you don't believe in the Bible or religion, self-love is our foundation as humans. I mean self-love, not narcissism. People who love themselves are authentic. They are self-aware, whole, fully single, and capable of sharing themselves. They know who they really are and accept their own insecurities. People who love themselves are honest about what they want and what they don't want.

CHAPTER 17

SOME QUICK RED FLAGS

At the beginning of any relationship, if you find yourself justifying the other person's behavior for any reason, stop and reflect on why. The mind can sometimes automatically rationalize things and paint a different picture if you have developed a habit of doing so. Or sometimes the mind can subconsciously discard things that don't align with your views if you've already set your perspective on a person. Sometimes, you may justify bad behavior for a person if you know some things about their past. You may say they are doing this because they went through that, or they went through this red flag.

If at the beginning of a relationship, you find that the person you are with won't talk through issues or doesn't know how to handle disagreements without walking away, shutting down, or blowing up—red flag.

Let's say at the beginning of a relationship, you discover that the person you're dealing with feels entitled and is comfortable with using other people because they don't care. It will be only a matter of time before you become one of those other people—red flag.

At the beginning of a relationship, if you find the person, you're dealing with is overly critical and seeks perfection from you or constantly criticizes and dismisses you, red flag.

When you get the feeling there's something wrong or there are many secrets; when the person isn't open or isn't honest; when there are unexplained behaviors, unnecessary blaming, or uncalled-for reactions to small things; and when you receive confusing explanations along with hurtful behavior, you already know—the uncalled-force are red flags. Our gut feeling is almost always right, Listen to it.

CHAPTER 18

PREPARATION MET WITH OPPORTUNITY IS A SUCCESS.

---

be Prepared

Today's culture has revealed for many years that people are not prepared to find good people as partners. Sometimes, it's because they are not good people themselves. Most of the time, it's because people don't have the correct information, the right mindset, and a clear understanding of what it takes to share a healthy, compatible lifestyle. Practice becoming self-aware and single so you will become whole enough to recognize a good person.

I believe that, if you follow the steps in this book, you will become and find the right fit for you! The first step is self-awareness. Start a relationship being whole and single before you start searching and start the interview process.

When you start the interview process, there are certain questions for you and your intended mate, the answers to which describe what you both believe, how you both behave, and what you both want. The next step in the interview is to ask your intended mate certain questions that reveal your compatible traits. And the last step in the interview process is to analyze how the intended mate describes how he or she deals with stress, challenges, and difficulties; how he or she thinks and acts; and whether those answers are compatible with yours. But first, you need "the talk."

Darrell Canty

the talk: Money, cheating, child-rearing, social media

At this point, most people who have read and practiced all the advice laid out. *How to Find the Perfect Love* in its planned order should feel pretty good about starting a healthy, completely confident relationship and very self-assured about how to find a perfect fit for them. I call this section "The Talk," because most people in relationships never have this talk. Even if you aren't self-aware, whole, and completely single and aren't prepared for a real-life's relationship journey. I believe the talk is necessary and can help anyone. The talk is about discovering why a person truly wants to attach their life to another person's life (your life). If you think you are ready to get serious with someone, you must have the talk first.

Find out why you and the other person want to be attached and somewhat accountable to one another, and why you want to share most of your things, space, money, and time. You're about to embark on a never-ending sleepover, dealing with children or in-laws you may or may not like, and depending on someone else to make the daily decisions that may directly affect you and your life's situation. Be clear about how you both want your household to run. I'm not talking about who washes the dishes and makes the bed. I'm referring to both of you agreeing or disagreeing that anyone can show up at any time to your home or that the children will be disciplined. Do we both feel comfortable with our friends and family going in and out of our house and refrigerator? Who makes the final decision? Things like that matter. Believe it or not, these little things can cause some big disturbances in your life.

The most important decision a couple will make other than having children is, why are we living together? Some reasons not to move in together include my lease being up, your house being closer to my job, it being too crowded where I'm at now, or I just need help. Be sure and have practical and healthy reasons for living together.

Money

It is a must you have "the money talk." Money, money, money is always a problem unless you address it before it becomes a problem. Moving in together means you will need to start managing money somewhat together. That doesn't mean you need to get a joint account; it means you both need to agree on how to share the expenses of the household. Make sure you are both on the same page about how you will spend, share, and save household money. It's imperative to talk about how each person feels about "my money" and "your money," as well as what things are important to them when it comes to how money is spent. It's important to know who will be financially responsible for what. It's important to talk about long-term possibilities. What will you do if one partner loses a job, or someone's car breaks down? If one person gains a large increase in income, what will you do with it?

All these things will affect the management of your money, and that will affect the management of your relationship. Be careful. Make sure there aren't red flags or big areas of disagreement when it comes to the management or spending of money. I believe money is the number one reason people break up in relationships. So be honest, respectful, and clear when having the money talk.

Cheating

If you are self-aware, whole, and successfully single and your partner is too, and you have a clear understanding of how you should share each other's body, emotions, and time, you should both agree on what is a healthy relationship, and cheating should never be an issue.

Cheating is very different between men and women Yes, it's true. A man usually will cheat for three reasons. This is because men aren't usually driven by their emotions, so cheating is usually not an emotional thing; it's an access thing, a distancing thing, an integrity thing. For any one of these reasons, a man will cheat. Lack of ownership (access, availability) from his partner may be the number one reason men cheat. Most men believe they have the right to you and your body once they commit to you. Even if you are not giving yourself to anyone else, it doesn't matter, if you aren't giving yourself to him. One of the men's favorite sayings is, "I can't have sex with anyone else, right?" I'm sure many women have heard this a time or two. When a man believes he doesn't have access to his significant other, this may cause him to cheat. Women sometimes use sex as a tool or weapon in their relationships. Women should always make themselves available for their men unless they are sick or experiencing an emotional tragedy or trauma in life. I'm not talking about bills, kids, and everyday stuff; I'm talking about a real tragedy. Try to always have the attitude that you'll give him as much sex as he can handle. What! Making it hard for him to leave home and hard for him to stay away too long.

Another reason this can happen is simply bad integrity. These types of men had never decided not to cheat, good luck! Some men have a habit of being with multiple women, and that's that. But usually, men will let you know in the beginning one way or another—either with telltale signs or by straight-out letting you know you should see this behavior early in the relationship if you are aware, and these types of men shouldn't be on your radar if you are seeking a relationship.

The last reason a man will cheat is distancing. Stress and adversities of life's dealing may cause both not communicating and connecting on a regular basis, this can cause distance and may cause him to cheat. Or he may feel he is not appreciated or respected because of how you treat him this may cause distancing and can cause him to cheat.

A woman may cheat for multiple reasons. She could be lacking attention, affection, or romance. Perhaps she's constantly being disrespected, or the sex (feeling) is not like it was in the beginning or she's experiencing an emotional void. Sometimes it could be that you aren't living up to her hopes; perhaps you're not handling your financial responsibilities at home or your duties around the house. It could be anything. It could be that you spend too much time away from home because of your work. Maybe she feels she could have done better, and her man is consistently showing up short as compared to the potential she sees in him.

I strongly believe, if a man cherishes and contributes to his woman, she will not cheat—if she is self-aware, whole, and single before they meet. To cherish her is to make her feel like she is the most important person in the world to you. I also, believe if a woman respects and gives herself to her man with complete access and availability, he will not cheat.

Therefore, it is a must that you both talk extensively about each other's needs, beliefs, and habits.

Child-Rearing

Believe it or not, child-rearing is high on the list of reasons marriages and relationships are breaking up today. Many couples create the myth of parental joy, not recognizing the huge sacrifice and investment children require. I also believe that couples who join families talk about raising children less than any other subject.

Raising children is difficult for any parent because it's emotionally and financially draining and involves day-to-day sacrifice. There are so many concerns people never think about until the child is already here.

These include questions like, how do we disciple the children? Who is responsible for taking them to the doctor and daily responsibilities? What choices should children have when it comes to their faith and religion? Children require so many things from their parents and families from the moment they are born. And this causes challenges for any individuals who aren't sure or clear on understanding how things will be done. With a lack of experience, lack of knowledge, and different perceptions, the challenges of raising children can be a nightmare. Furthermore, finances play the biggest part in these challenges. Lack of money brings a lack of choices and will affect the children, the situation, and the parents.

Social Media

Today most people live as much in their e-life as they do in real life. Social media has been a rising concern for many. This is because social media tends to allow people to connect with other people with ease and promotes a level of desired connection that leads to intimacy when sharing behaviors, attitudes, and beliefs. If someone isn't transparent about who's in a relationship using social media and the activities, he or she engages in on that platform with other people can cause suspicion. This can lead to distancing, anxiety, depression, stress, and violence. Many couples say social media is one of the biggest sources of jealousy and infidelity in their relationships. Many couples say social media is the main reason they feel threatened in their relationship. This behavior can cause them to search through their partner's stuff for evidence of cheating, virtual or otherwise. This behavior causes arguments and disagreements. Many times, secrets via social media accounts suggest bad behavior. It's becoming more and more frequent that couples find themselves fighting so often or having such a degree of doubt in their marriage or relationships because of what they've found on social media that can cause reason for separation.

Misconduct with people could lead to addiction to social media and, eventually, disrupt your current and future relationships. So, it is a necessity to have "the social media talk." Talk to your intended partner to understand his or her views, behaviors, and thoughts related to the use of social media and find out if you're like-minded on this issue before you commence. Talk about social media use in the beginning don't wait.

CHAPTER 19

WHY THE INTERVIEW

Everyone should have the interview before they commit to someone else. The interview should be done in the beginning stages before you've developed a strong liking for one another. Many people like to get with someone and later start learning, discovering, and changing their partner to fit them or their needs; that doesn't work. That's why people need a plan to interview. This process should eliminate many or all the pitfalls, people stumble into without getting the necessary information when they start a relationship. This entire process will determine how honest you and your intentions are when it comes to who you are and what you want. Remember, honesty is the most important quality with self and in any relationship. Honesty teaches us many lessons…

The more we practice honesty, the more we use modesty and uprightness with our words and actions. Honesty demonstrates how genuine and important we are to ourselves and to one another; I believe those who love with the best honesty are best at love, so be super honest. It's about being real with yourself and the other person—about who you are, what you want and need, and how you live. These interview questions are the best course to initiate a relationship and provide you with confidence that you have enough important information to start trusting in who your intended partner is.

There are many people who believe that God chooses our mate. I know, but God doesn't pick people's mates because of free will. If He decided to surpass our free will and choose our mate, wouldn't

He choose our salvation instead? So, let's not take a chance on our future partner without exercising practical sense, compatibility, and the interview process. This way we wouldn't need to make whomever we choose to fit us later. "We married now!"

The interview process may be one of the most effective ways to ensure you're both qualified to be in a relationship together. Even if you're not a complete person, the interview and understanding compatibility can help you choose the best possible person to fit you.

People must be qualified to drive a car or motorcycle, build a house, start certain businesses, and on and on. But society says it's not necessary for a person to be qualified for you to spend your life with him or her (to create a life together, no requirements needed) Wow!

Make sure you and your intended are successfully single before you engage in a relationship for both of your good. For the best results, you want to be sure your intended partner is already equipped with the basic life tools we've discussed and is independent, resilient, and practical when it comes to dealing with life's challenges. For the first serval months watch them and their choices and behavior. Of course, everyone won't be at the same level because of life experiences and the fact that we're all individual people, who hurt. If you both have most of what you need to link up according to the information in this book, you'll be fine. I recommend you don't move in together until you both are self-aware, whole, and single for at least for one year.

Let's get started with the interview process.

CHAPTER 20

THE INTERVIEW PROCESS (PROFILING)

Hello!

This is one of my favorite parts of the book, although to get the complete ammunition for the interview process and the best understanding of compatibility attend one of our workshops coming soon go to greatvalue4us.com. Most people have accepted there is no sure way to discover whether you and an intended mate are truly compatible. There is hope.

Before people build a house, they make sure the ground beneath is firm and solid. Basically, before you get started in a relationship, make sure you establish a good foundation for the best results. This is part of the interview process. Develop and confirm both person's foundations are sound and identify a person's philosophy and behaviors. The fact we humans are social creatures living in an imperfect world with many different values, conflicting beliefs, and actions affects us for the good and the bad. Sometimes having a right to our own opinion is very important; it sometimes makes us believe our opinion is always right.

During the first part of the interview process, you're looking to see how your intended partner's principles align with your principles. Also, you're looking to discover how practical he or she is when it comes to dealing with conflict, changes, and challenges. The next part of the interview process asks additional questions that connect you to how compatible you and your intentions are related to long-term and future expectations. Make sure you see the planned areas that demonstrate a compatible direction with yours.

Ask questions to your would-be partners to describe themselves in terms of how they think and behave in certain situations of stress and difficulty. Have them comment on how their family members and friends think of them or see them and why. Ask them about their flaws or things they would change about themselves. Ask them if there are areas they need to improve on. Ask questions to find out what frustrates them and how they handle that frustration. Ask questions like, what are some things that would influence you to stay in or leave a relationship? Ask them what important things that are known to be true about men and women can help facilitate a healthy relationship. Ask them to describe the best part of themselves. Ask them, what are some difficult decisions you have made in the past to improve a relationship? You want to ask as many questions as you need to determine your intended partner's experiences and behavior to understand the other person's values and way of moving through life and see if it fits with yours.

Try to find out a potential partner's belief system and how it would align with yours. Determine whether you're each seeking marriage or not. Find out your potential partner's perspective on relationships and whether you share the same beliefs about family, friends, and self-worth. Another important foundational element is determining whether your intended mate considers his or her partner first above and before other family members as a priority when dealing with relationship challenges.

This next set of questions is intended to determine how a person responds to challenges and conflicts. Determine what strategies he or she employs in conflict. Find out what life experiences have led him or her to behave in certain ways in certain situations, and whether the approach allows for a healthy planned outcome. These questions should be designed to demonstrate how a person behaves and to identify domestic problems and issues before they become crises. They should reveal how well your intended deals with many different conflicts and difficulties.

The last set of questions helps you recognize compatible behaviors and habits that align with your approaches and attitudes toward life. These questions are designed to demonstrate a person's position and ideas that are supportive and can be a benefit to yours, or not. Through asking them these questions, you'll discover if there are compatible behaviors that will allow the two of you to align yourselves together and support one another in daily interactions. Be clear when you are determining the lifestyle you want to lead. This section should include questions like, do you smoke? Do you gamble? Inquire into other vices a potential partner may have that won't disturb or conflict with your behavior or lifestyle values. You should include additional questions that may reveal more about the person's rational thinking and actions in day-to-day situations. These questions should include how flexible and open-minded your potential partner is.

Other than the way a person looks, we have designed a detailed set of questions and a complete profile process you can retrieve with our workshops to find a good match for you. There too, you'll find a compatibility test, which clearly reveals and demonstrates the closest possible match between two people. With twenty-seven years of research and development, we took the guess out of guessing.

To access the complete Interview and Compatibility workshop, please go to wwwgreatvalue4uscom to learn more and "Find Your Perfect Fit."

CHAPTER 21

THE SHORT STORY

Many people spend much of their lives looking for that "one." Some people have spent too much time searching for the one and not enough time building up themselves. If you don't spend the right amount of time on yourself, you will always be short of what you need and what you can give. Don't find someone you have to hang in there with. You hang in there with your children; you hang in there with your job. With your partner, find someone whom you find it hard to stay away from. Find someone with whom you see so many benefits of sharing their space, time, and lifestyle. But don't hang in there with someone that's not a good fit. Don't settle with anyone, and don't settle for being anything less than for someone else. The primary focus when seeking a partner is to look for someone you like, just the way he or she is. If you like all the good and the bad, even if the good never gets any better and the bad never goes away, you're good. If that's not the person, then that's not the person. Have a mindset that asks, what can I bring to the relationship to make the bond better, rather than, what do I need from someone to help me make it through my situation? People should enter a bond with the desire not to fix, correct, or change anything about the other person. Say to yourself, if he or she doesn't change a thing, I'll be satisfied. Being a whole person is being self-centered with the will to share without feeling the loss of any contributions you give, why? Because you are willing and able.

Intimate relationships aren't supposed to come about by chance or based on a chemical connection (sexual attraction). We aren't supposed to be spending days, months, or years to make our relationships work. Truly healthy relationships aren't based on compromise or fifty-fifty give-and-take. Sustainable relationships aren't based on the idea that, if the other person does his or her part, I'll do my part. Long-lasting, intimate relationships develop when two individuals discover an honest, clear awareness, with balance and a deliberate decision about shared motives, aligned principles, and a desire to please the other, and each person is his or her true self (no changes needed!).

With all relationships, success or failure is predictable. It's no mystery. Failure comes when one or both partners choose to tolerate unhealthy behavior or ignore it or participate in it. Failure comes with a lack of self-awareness and the work done on yourself. When partners aren't whole as individuals and when they don't share core values and compatible lifestyles, that invites failure.

Success in relationships has to do with connecting principles and shared behaviors, not conditioned to the other. This goes along with both partners having the right mindset, the correct information about each other, and a clear understanding of themselves and their insecurities. And it includes sharing a compatible lifestyle, not just interests or commonalities. Many seem to choose what is easiest.

CHAPTER 22

FOR MEN

For men who don't believe they should provide, lead, protect, or give to their woman, shame on you. If you are in a relationship, that's what it is. When a man does not establish his spiritual self (not his religious self) and only relies completely on his human self, he is limited and incomplete—unable to be the head, the leader, or the foundation he was intended to be. All people are spiritually governed by their natural aspects of goodness, passion, and greed. So, men who don't have higher accountability and a spiritual foundation will never fully become who they were designed to become and will fail by their own thoughts and behavior, consistently returning to rely on their limited understanding. So, develop and continue to develop your self-awareness. Learn the natural way to drive your beliefs, views, and choices that form and develop your personality and enable you to become the best version of yourself. Become the leader you were designed to be. A true leader of his home doesn't have to ask his woman to follow him She wants to follow him.

For men, women in relationships are designed to co-depend on the substance of a good man. A good man knows his strengths and can admit to his weaknesses. If a man does not establish his foundation and his know-how about his woman's needs, he will lose. When a man has a solid foundation of self and his inner spirit, he has what is needed to lead, provide, and protect his partner and family and to manage his fundamentals and behavior to overcome any emotional challenges and his own internal barriers first. Being a complete man requires achieving your own self-fulfillment through a spiritual foundation and correct attitude, as well as developing economic and physical discipline. This is done while prioritizing your life and achieving your goals. A woman depends on and needs a foundation and companion who puts her needs before his own. This is natural. A woman needs the moral integrity of a man even if she doesn't have her own; he will increase hers. Women need relational compassion and emotional intimacy from a man who doesn't center his self-esteem around a woman but on his principles, Stay with me.

For men, always be honest with your woman and be open. A woman needs this to be fully comfortable and give herself wholly to you. Men study your woman. The more you know about her nature and behavior, the more relaxed, calm, and easy it will be for her to give herself to you. Another truth for you men—women never get enough I know, I know; it's by design. So, give, give, and keep giving to your woman because they were designed to receive, receive, and keep on receiving. A wise man would not get angry at a tree that does what a tree is supposed to do or a dog for doing dog things. My point is a woman's nature is to receive and always receive. Her body is designed to receive, her mind is designed to receive, and her emotions are all intended to receive. So, don't get angry when she wants, wants, and wants. When a woman wants things, she just is in her element. I didn't say give her everything she wants; give her what she needs. Just don't expect her not to want more. So, give her body attention with your eyes, hands, words, and body. Give her mind words of encouragement, comfort, and assurance that she is valuable to you. Give her emotions the security that you are responsible in your actions and responsible with your words. Be accountable with your commitments; share your time with action; recognize her contributions; and continue to give deeds and gifts, as she is designed to receive them.

For men, women need affection like men need respect. If a woman doesn't get what she needs, she will malfunction. Affection for a woman is a man's words and touch, as well as his care. Women crave a man's affection and personal devotion (his time), so they'll feel cared for, set aside, and special. Affection for a woman is holding, hugging, kissing, holding hands, and especially hearing from her man the precious words of how good and sexy she looks and how much he cares for and loves her.

CHAPTER 23

FOR WOMEN

For women who aren't self-aware or concerned about their lack of control, expressing their emotions without shame, dignity, and respect, shame on you. For women who pressure their husbands or significant others to do what they can't handle or give what they can't afford shame on you. For women who want him to become what she believes he should be, shame on you. These women are a significant part of our failed community. When a woman is not focused and concerned about developing herself as a virtuous woman, she invites a structure of chaos into her life and usually a broken home and absent fathers for their kids that adds to our broken community. Finding a virtuous woman, one who is valuable and brings good to her man, family, and herself and is respected by all is rare.

A virtuous woman does not tear down her man or her house with her tongue without limits. A virtuous woman is a helper, a giver, and a producer in anything she is involved in. She encourages and builds her family, friends, and neighbors with her words and her actions. A virtuous woman knows it is not realistic for her husband or significant other to meet all her emotional needs. A virtuous woman knows that any argument always starts with herself and doesn't depend on how she feels, but rather acts in a practical manner based on what happened. A virtuous woman doesn't take her vision and separate it from her man's vision, causing division; she combines her vision with his. A virtuous woman believes her emotional support comes from God, herself, and the environment she creates and not from other people. A virtuous woman makes her home inviting, warm, and safe for her man to come home to. A virtuous woman guards her tongue.

For women, the biggest part of getting what you want from a man is knowing how to convey those wants so that he will understand. For example, if things around the house aren't getting done and she needs help, she can't just say to the man, "I need help." He doesn't know what that means. She needs to ask for a specific thing, like, "Please clean the kitchen and put your clothes in the laundry room." If they come home together from a night out and she sees things out of place, she may automatically assume he sees the house the same way. Most often, he will not. And if it is a concern, this needs to be communicated, not escalated. A virtuous woman directs her thoughts and guards her tongue.

For women, after you have been with your man for a while, sometimes your emotions may start to lead you into chaos, Stop. For example, let's say your weight is one of your emotional problems. If your man is not complaining, disrespecting, or concerned about the weight you may have gained or loss, don't hold that against him. Stay away from the media's expectations and society's demands of what is right or acceptable. In other words, if he is still into you and wants you *regardless* of how you feel about him, let him have it; as a matter of fact, give it to him. I mean you should give him as much sex and as much of you as he can handle, while you work on you. Don't let your weight issues or any of your issues put a wedge between you and him. Remember that's your issue. Go back to the self-love section and love yourself. You can still work on your issues if they remain a concern to you. Women, all the time, when possible, you should love on (have sex with) your man; do it so much that he doesn't have the energy or desire for another woman. Men need sex and respect like women need affection and attention. An unlimited amount of sex and no respect, means nothing. Respect comes first. Please hear me. We need to give each other what we need.

For women, most people believe a man needs sex as his priority. This isn't true. Respect is the most important quality to give a man, period. If you offer a man all the sex he can handle and no respect, this won't make him want you or respect you. But he will still take all that sex because sex is sex to a man. It's hard for a man to be intimate with his woman if she tears him down with her words. To respect a man is to admire his knowledge and opinion and value his decisions. Men especially don't like judgment and being questioned on their decisions in a relationship. If you truly love (*respect*) him, sometimes you need to recognize that whatever decisions he makes, whether good or bad, he's doing if it is for both of your interests, leave it alone. Yes, leave it alone (close your mouth).

Women, you cannot pick a man. Stop. Even if you pick a man. In other words, if you choose a man before he chooses you, he is not yours. A man who gives in to a woman he is not ready for, or he did not choose is not truly hers. He may be sleeping in her bed, eating her food, and driving her car, but he still isn't yours. Only when a man chooses you will your union be genuine. A woman shouldn't pursue or chase a man in any way because it is by natural design. By natural design, a man's nature is to always chase after a woman by his eyes, her attitude, and her femininity. So, women, stop looking for a man, stop trying to get him to commit, and prepare yourself to be rare—rare like a virtuous woman. As a woman, you can only hope to find a good man by being self-aware, fully single, and whole. Start practicing how to guard your tongue, enhance your attributes, and build up your character. Finding a unique man means being prepared emotionally and physically and developing healthy behaviors. Finding a unique man—a man who wants to provide, protect, and cultivate; a man who provides spiritual guidance, economic security, emotional support.

Women need a man who can manage his household, a man who protects his family's emotional stability and his family's whole foundation while he cultivates himself and his family.

Any man who can't add and improve a woman is not ready for a woman. Any woman who can't guard her tongue and doesn't know how to respect a man is not ready for a man.

CHAPTER 24

THE SUMMARY

How to Find the Perfect Love

I'm assuming I'm writing this part to a woman. Don't be obsessed with finding sex, love, or romance. After you have a sense of self and have set your priorities, you can put some effort into finding a real connection with someone. It's OK to join social groups and attend single events. Be focused when you put yourself out there. Seek compatibility, not romance. Remember, you're looking for compatibility first because it doesn't matter how attracted you are to each other if you're not compatible. One of the biggest key components in attracting people is feeling good about yourself and having a good attitude. So set your foundation with positive thoughts daily, a healthy environment, and uplifting friends and family around you. Most of the time positive, self-confident people attract all types of people and opportunities. Instant sexual attraction always fades. Find someone you like because of their character and how their life aligns with your life. When you build a slow and long-lasting attraction, it will be much more sustainable.

Please don't believe the theory that "opposites attract"; even if they do, they don't fit well together. Start all your interest and engagements with honest and transparent behavior. That way, you'll get what you want whether you're just fooling around or it's a real relationship.

Before you start looking, understand your own needs and behavior. Know when someone is unavailable by listening not only with your ears because they will show you. Women seem to be the problem with maintaining sexual desire in a relationship because they seem to get disinterested a lot sooner than men. So, you need to tell him whatever it is you need to keep your motor running; consistently remind him. Women try not to gravitate to the romance that leads to sex but, rather, to the attraction to your man. Women, please believe this when I say men are simple and simple-minded. All that means is tell your man everything you want, like, don't like, and so on. Sometimes you may have to repeat yourself; no worries Don't leave it up to him to figure it out. He won't! I strongly believe that, when the two of you are compatible, chemistry can be created and become stronger. Because you are so connected just by virtue of who you are, there can be a stronger chemistry attraction and understanding of one another's needs.

Women keep in mind if you truly want to find the perfect love, you must stop focusing on your education, economic position, and your self-interest and focus on getting your man. That may sound bad, but men usually aren't seeking long-term relationships even if they want one. Also, men don't care about your educational position and economic status especially if you are not wanting to contribute significantly financially after you guys are together. This all points to becoming self-aware and increasing your self-value for a good man.

Be empowered by this information and use the tools shared in *How to Find the Perfect Love* to handle conflict and difficulties in your relationship. Hopefully, this book has delivered a clear understanding and given you a spot-on path of action to reveal the true way to relate to self and one another. A true, long, and successful relationship means always wanting and being willing to put the other person first. Love your partner as Jesus loves you. Stay focused "Love is a choice that creates feeling, not a feeling that causes you to choose." —DC

The relationship we all want,
Is in the ones who know how they affect themselves and others.

—DC

Chapter by chapter, author Darrell Canty constructs a familiar picture of common behavior that reveals a pattern and history of misinformation and lack of understanding. The new "do you" paradigm leads men and women to connect in unnatural ways in relationships that produce a steady track record of failure and disaster. Discover a new way to find a broken person who's the perfect fit.

How to Find the Perfect Love reveals a snapshot of how people have been conditioned to think and act when behaving in relationships. It also provides a clear, healthy way to prevent the traps of the media's way of condoning these unhealthy ways people are involved in relationships. In addition, the author hands you the blueprint to a fruitful, fulfilling, and healthy way of dealing with and overcoming distractions and dysfunction while engaging in and maintaining a good relationship.

The author identifies how he believes the Creator's original plan for men and women was intended to be. This type of relationship starts with the individual and his or her spiritual self. We need to understand the relationship between ourselves and the Creator and the Creator's relationship with us.

Whether you believe it or not, we can choose the perfect fit for a partner, which will in turn become our perfect love. Love is a choice, and choices can be predictable based on situations, circumstances and passed behavior. Allow *How to Find the Perfect Love* to direct you there—to your one love.

Printed in the United States
by Baker & Taylor Publisher Services